The Obvious Child

Studies in the Significance of Childhood

Roger Neustadter

University Press of America,® Inc.
Lanham · Boulder · New York · Toronto · Plymouth, UK

Copyright © 2009 by
University Press of America,® Inc.
4501 Forbes Boulevard
Suite 200
Lanham, Maryland 20706
UPA Acquisitions Department (301) 459-3366

Estover Road
Plymouth PL6 7PY
United Kingdom

Library of Congress Control Number: 2008936383
ISBN-13: 978-0-7618-4365-8 (clothbound : alk. paper)
ISBN-10: 0-7618-4365-5 (clothbound : alk. paper)
ISBN-13: 978-0-7618-4366-5 (paperback : alk. paper)
ISBN-10: 0-7618-4366-3 (paperback : alk. paper)
eISBN-13: 978-0-7618-4367-2
eISBN-10: 0-7618-4367-1

∞™The paper used in this publication meets the minimum
requirements of American National Standard for Information
Sciences—Permanence of Paper for Printed Library Materials,
ANSI Z39.48—1984

For Danny and Dave
who taught me that the sky is not the sky

CONTENTS

Acknowledgments

Portions of this work have been previously published, in different form, in the following journals: "The Politics of Growing Up: The Status of Childhood in Modern Social Thought, *Current Perspectives in Social Theory*, Volume 9, pages 1999-2211989 by JAI Press Inc; "Phone Home: From Childhood Amnesia to the Catcher in Sci-Fi—The Transformation of Childhood in Contemporary Science Fiction Films," *Youth & Society*, Vol. 20 No. 3 March 1989, pages 227-240, Sage Publications, Inc.

INTRODUCTION

The simple fact that there are so many children and that children are a part of so many contemporary issues might lead one to expect that there would be many scholarly studies of children both in the past and in the present. Children have been ubiquitous. Their numbers alone have made them a force in history and society. Yet, in the very academic disciplines such as history, sociology, and literature in which one might expect a focus on children and childhood there has been until recently conspicuously little attention devoted to children and childhood.

The study of childhood is coming of age. There is a new era of childhood and subsequently of childhood studies. As Steinberg and Kincheloe (1997, 1) have observed "New times have ushered in a new era of childhood. Evidence of this dramatic cultural change surrounds each of us." Once overlooked and viewed as a trivial subject of interest only to arcane specialists, the overlooked child has become the obvious child, now part of the cutting edge of disciplinary and interdisciplinary scholarship. For sometime now the academic spotlight has begun to focus on childhood. New and important theoretical and empirical work has been done by a number of scholars who advocate the conceptual autonomy of children and childhood (Corsaro, 1997; Steinberg and Kincheloe, 1997). The significance of children and childhood has become obvious and compelling to scholars in many disciplines. Such works focus on children as the basic units and categories of study.

Children have increasingly been separated out as a special case when speaking of economic, social problems and political problems such as child poverty, child prostitution, and child labor. In part this is because children have emerged as a significant population in themselves, and in part this is because by demonstrating the terrible impact that these phenomena have on children people are invited to care about these areas of human misery. Children and childhood have become the center of research and the center of attention in themselves. Many new works (Kenny, 2007; Kirsh, 2006; Schor 2004) focus on the status of children as the basic category of study.

Evidence of the new era of childhood and interpretation of this dramatic change is evident in the emerging status of children and childhood in both society and culture. There are now several texts on the Sociology of Childhood. There is a growing volume of scholarship in many disciplines which centers on the significance and importance of children in history, culture and society. The purpose of this book is to examine the conceptual autonomy of childhood in several areas of society and culture. The essays in this book attempt to examine the significance of childhood in a number of specific areas of society and culture. The book is organized into two parts. Part I focuses on the status of children in several locations and institutions of society. The chapters in this section deal with the status of children and childhood in historiography, in social theory, in the courtroom, and in the media. Part II focuses on the status and the importance of children and childhood as they are represented in popular culture. The chapters in this section deal with the status of children and childhood in utopian literature, science fiction films, popular music, and contemporary memoirs. The Epilogue looks at several emerging social issues involving children.

PART I
The Transformation of the Child in Society

CHAPTER ONE
The Historical Child

In looking back through history we often assume that our present attitudes and behaviors are "normal," and judge others on the basis of what seems "natural." Childhood in the United States and most Western societies has been seen as a special phase in the life cycle, set apart from adulthood. The modern concept of childhood suggests that children must be stringently safeguarded, must receive a proper education, and that only after many years of moral, physical, and intellectual quarantine can they be allowed to join adults. Childhood is treated as a unique period in life because of prevailing beliefs that children are different from adults; that is children are believed to be more innocent, less capable of evil, and therefore more in need of protection, careful direction, and training. That the treatment of children and perceptions of childhood in the past has not been the present projected backward has been the subject of several "historical revisionist" studies based on "new evidence."

In a number of recent and fascinating works several important scholars have come to the conclusion that the concept of childhood that prevails in contemporary Western civilization is largely a product of the past few centuries. They hold that the attitudes of adults toward children as well as the actual lives of children were inherently and categorically different from those in the modern West. Slowly, at a pace which varied from class to class, country to country, and even family to family, they contend, there took place a remarkable change in the social status of childhood and in affective relations between parents and children. What emerged was the "modern" concept of childhood, in which childhood was viewed as a unique stage of life separate from adulthood.

The history of childhood has become an embattled topic. For those endeavoring to understand the lives of children in the past problems of evidence (quantitative and qualitative; indirect evidence and primary sources) and interpretation have combined to render the history of childhood an area of inquiry rife with controversy. The scholars who have studied the status of childhood in the past are not in total agreement on all the important features of the way childhood existed in the past, or the variables that led to the transformation from a time when there was no childhood to the present. Interpretations of the history of childhood have varied considerably. Of the numerous studies which have focused on examining the status of childhood in the past two distinctive descriptions of the status of childhood in the past emerge. One interpretation of the status of childhood in the past views children as having occupied a congenial relationship with society and adults. The second interpretation argues that in the past children were not valued and were mistreated. Philippe Aries (1962) is the foremost proponent of the former interpretation. Lloyd de Mause is the foremost proponent of the later interpretation.

According to Aries children were happy in the past, particularly during the Middle Ages. Because society was not preoccupied with raising the young and severely restricting their lives conditions for children were relatively good. Communal living brought people of all ages together more as natural companions than as uniquely different kinds of beings. De Mause by contrast, interprets child-raising practices in Freudian psychological terms and concludes that, while some parents in history may have loved their children; most parents were emotionally immature and lodged at a lower stage of human development. De Mause believes that child raising in the past, which featured infanticide, abandonment, and abuse was a blot on the history of civilization.

This chapter is devoted to examining how historians such as Aries and de Mause, and those who have been inspired by, or support the work of each of these historians, have described the change in the status of childhood, and how they have explained the historical transformation of childhood from the past to the present. This chapter will first describe the work of Aries and other historians who see society's attitude toward children in the past as an attitude of indifference in which children were congenially assimilated into the social world of adults. Then the chapter examines de Mause and the work of other historians who see the existence of childhood in the past as one of systematic mistreatment and abuse in which children were frequently subject to neglect and cruelty. After elaborating the different descriptions of the status of childhood in the past this chapter will examine several of the explanations of this transformation of childhood.

The Assimilation of Children into Society

The most influential book on childhood in the past is *Centuries of Childhood* by Philippe Aries (1962). In *Centuries* Aries attempted to refocus the interest of historians on the powerless and inarticulate members of society whose experiences and lives had been overlooked by traditional historians because they did not leave written records. Convinced that history should be more than the history of elites, Aries attempted to construct a history that included the historical experiences of people regardless of class, gender, race, or age. Aries held that the past was a period in which children were treated with indifference, their lives incorporated into the world of adults. Aries argued that there was no concept of childhood before the seventeenth century; as soon as children could leave the care of the nursery, they entered the adult world.

Aries questioned the notion that any constructed social space for childhood existed in the medieval world, claiming that there was no distinctive "idea" of childhood in the past. Early infancy was recognized only to be followed by a period of miniature adulthood, in which adults and children shared the same world—a world in which few significant social distinctions between children and adults were drawn. Aries argues that until recently the world of childhood was assimilated into the world of adults.

> In medieval society the idea of childhood did not exist; this is not to suggest that children were neglected, forsaken or despised. The idea of childhood is not to be confused with affection for children: it corresponds to an awareness of the particular nature of childhood, that particular nature which distinguishes the child from the adult, even the young adult. In medieval society this awareness was lacking. That is why, as soon as the child could live without the constant solicitude of his mother, his nanny or his cradle-rocker, he belonged to adult society (1962, 128).

Aries argues that the meaning of childhood underwent a gradual transformation in Europe from the twelfth to the eighteenth centuries. He contends that Western society moved from ignorance of childhood to the centering of the family around the child in nineteenth century. Aries finds significant evidence to support his contention that in the past children once out of infancy mingled freely with adults. Aries and his epigone point to a number of markers which suggest that in the past childhood as a status did not exist, and that children were incorporated into the world of adults.

The proponents of this perspective contend that until the last several hundred years the world of representation was one in which childhood was unknown. Among the surviving statutes of the Greeks, Neil Postman notes, none was that of a child (Postman, 1982, 6). In the sixteenth and seventeenth centuries, Aries holds, most people regarded children merely as miniature adults, with the same responsibilities and capabilities as their elders. Examining the iconography of the middle ages he claimed that:

> Medieval art until about the twelfth century did not know childhood nor did not attempt to portray it. It is hard to believe that this neglect was due to incompetence or incapacity; it seems more probably that there was no place for childhood in the medieval world (1962, 33).

In numerous paintings Aries describes the "deformation" that artists of the twelfth century "inflict on children's bodies" (1962, 33). Children were painted with the musculature of adults. Artists, he argues, used the anatomic proportions of adults; they painted children with heads a sixth of the length of bodies instead of a quarter the length of their bodies. "In the tenth century," he observed "artists were unable to depict a child except as a man on a smaller scale" (1962, 10). Children occupied the same social space as adults. Often children were painted in groups and gatherings with adults in everyday life for the purposes of work, leisure, and sport (1962, 37). Thus children were depicted as gambling and going to such activities as horse races.

The world of children is not differentiated from the world of adults by those who lived during the Middle Ages. Aries found no portrait of children in the unique moments of their lives. Children were absent, Aries points, out from certain moments in the lives of families:

> No one thought of keeping a picture of a child if that child had either lived to grow to manhood or had died infancy. In the first case, childhood was simply an unimportant phase of which there was no need to keep any record; in the second case, that of the dead child, it was thought that the little thing which had disappeared so soon in life was not worthy of remembrance: there were far too many children whose survival was problematical (1962, 38).

Such emotional distancing from the child Aries suggests was natural in the community conditions of the time.

The apparent absence of bereavement in the face of an infant's death further underlines the point. Until the eighteenth century in Europe, the death of an infant or a young child was felt to be a minor event, met with a mixture of indifference and resignation. As Montaigne remarked, "I have lost two or three children in infancy, not with regret, but without great sorrow"(qtd. in Zelizer, 1985, 24). Parents seldom attended their child's funeral. In some sections of France, according Aries the child who died "too soon," was probably buried in the backyard, as cat or dog was buried. At death, even the children of the rich were treated as paupers, the bodies "sewn into shrouds made of cheap sacking and thrown into big common graves" (1962, 40).

Similarly Lawrence Stone, in his investigation of the English family, found no evidence of the purchase of symbols of mourning, not even an arm band, when a very young child died in the sixteenth, seventeenth and early eighteenth centuries. Children even though interred in family crypts were not recorded on the tombs when they died in infancy (Stone, 1979, 257). Parents seldom attended their child's funeral. Stone also notes that the omission from genealogies of "very short lived infants among the children of the aristocracy"(1979, 257).

The child was such an "unimportant little thing" Stone notes that not only was no memorabilia retained of the dead child, but the use of the name of a deceased or even a living child within a family was a common practice. During the middle ages and the sixteenth century, it had been common practice to give a new-born child the same first name as an elder sibling. Edward Gibbon recorded that after his birth in 1737, that his condition was so feeble that his family successively repeated the Christian name of Edward for a younger sibling in case of the departure of the eldest son (1979, 257).

Western culture did not have the language capacity to acknowledge the social recognition of childhood. Childhood was not noteworthy in its own right. Many languages lacked words to distinguish babies from those who are now called adolescents. The old adage, Neil Postman notes, that the Greeks had word for everything seemingly did not apply to the concept of childhood. Their words for youth and infancy ambiguously include almost anyone between infancy and old age (Postman, 1982, 6). It was not until the eighteenth century Aries contends that the terms used to denote childhood became both common and modern. Language did not give the word "child" the restricted meaning it is given today. Aries notes that some languages did not even include words to describe childhood and the meaning of age:

> ...in its attempts to talk about little children, the French language of the seventeenth century was hampered by the lack of words to distinguish them from bigger ones. This was true of English where the word 'baby' was also applied to big children...People had no idea of what we call adolescence, and the idea was a long time taking shape (1962:28–29).

It is not until the 18th century, Aries holds; largely through borrowing words form other languages that French and other European languages fully develop a vocabulary for describing infancy, childhood, and adolescence as separate and distinct periods of development.

The marked indifference shown to children before the seventeenth century was not confined to the world of pictures and words. The clothing of children also is a marker of the way that childhood was indistinguishable from adulthood. Aries found that the clothing of the period was similar for children and adults; "As soon as the child abandoned his swaddling band— the band of cloth that was wound tightly round his body in babyhood—he was dressed just like the other men and women of his class" (1962, 50). The Middle Ages dressed children very indiscriminately, taking care only to maintain signs of the social class hierarchy. This can be seen in paintings where the artists gave little indication of the ages of children. Thus, in a painting by Philippe de Champaign a boy "at ten is already dressed like a little man wrapped in a cloak; in appearance at least, he belongs to the world of adults" (1962, 51) A difference in dress was not to be found among girls either, "who; were dressed like little women as soon as they came out of their swaddling clothes" (1962,53). Children were not separated from adults by a uniform or clothing designating their special social status.

Aries claims that the recreational activities of children were also collapsed into the world of adult activities. A common conclusion drawn by those who study toys is that in the past they usually began as something that adults used and were then passed to children after their practical value had ended. Aries noted that the young and old played the same games. Before 1600:

> ...the specialization of games and pastimes did not extend beyond infancy; after the age of three or four it decreased and disappeared. From then on the child played the same games as the adult, either with other children or with adults...People had no objection to allowing children to play card games and games of chance, and to play for money (1962, 71).

Aries points out that numerous paintings of the period showed adults and children watching games of dice, wrestling, and horse racing.

Aries also found little evidence of a concern with protecting the moral innocence of children. In a fascinating series of excerpts from the diaries of Heroard who was the physician of King Henry IV of France, Aries documents the sexual familiarity and the inclusion of children in the sexual lives of the adult members of the aristocracy. According to Heroard's diary Henry's young son Louis XIII was seen as a sexual figure by whom adults were amused:

> He laughed uproariously when his nanny waggled his cock with her fingers. An amusing trick which the child soon copies. Calling a page, he shouted, 'Hey there!' and pulled up his robe, showing him his cock (1962, 100).

Members of the royal family also played immodestly with children. Aries cites numerous calendars, church pictures, and other forms of art in which children were commonly shown urinating in public places or mothers were shown breast feeding children (1962, 105–106). Aries suggests that this kind of behavior and this kind of familiarity between males and females of all ages were due not just to communal living arrangements, but to a set of cultural norms in which little distinction was made between adults and children, which made children socially acceptable and easily assimilated into the social world of adults.

Despite high death rates Aries held, it was precisely because society was not preoccupied with raising the young and severely restricting their lives that conditions for children were relatively good and their lives happy and sociable. Lloyd de Mause, by contrast interprets child raising practices in Freudian psychological terms. Unable to the view the child as a person separate from themselves, he claims, parents projected on their children all their own evil impulses of which they were possessed. In contrast to Aries, de Mause believes that child raising practices were repressive and the lives of children in the past a "nightmare." He depicts a world in children were adjudged not to be little adults, but worthless and troublesome, and frequently subject to neglect and cruelty.

The Nightmare of Childhood

Philippe Aries work on the social history of childhood has been challenged in recent years by the psycho historian Lloyd de Mause who claims that the "history of childhood is a nightmare from which we have only recently begun to awaken" and that the further back in history we delve, the worse the levels of brutality and terror for children. Historical evidence of brutality leads de Mause and others to a thesis directly opposed to that of Aries: that the past is a series of atrocities for children in which children were brutalized. The evidence they uncover for their position serves to paint a grim and somber picture of cruelty to children throughout the ages.

De Mause argues for a psychoanalytic reading of childhood history and attempts to analyze the psychological principles that have characterized child/adult relations. The parents described by Aries were not harsh or cruel parents, merely indifferent ones who had little interest in their children and saw little of them. The further back in history one goes de Mause contends, the lower the level of parental childcare, and the more likely children are to be killed, abandoned, beaten, terrorized and sexually abused. De Mause claimed that social historians such as Aries have conspired in an historical cover up by "playing down" the widespread brutality and cruelty to children in ages past hiding, distorting, softening, and ignoring masses of evidence to give a benign picture of childhood in the past (1974, 21). Other historians also paint a dreary picture of childhood in the past. Edward Shorter (1977) describes a past not only without love between husband and wife, but between parents and children. Lawrence Stone has also concluded that the historical treatment of children is a "catalogue of atrocities." "The cruel truth," he noted, "may be that most parents in history have not been much involved with their children, and have not cared much about them" (1974: 29).

De Mause constructs a psychogenic model in which he depicts adults in terms of three historical reactions—projective, reversal, and empathic. In the early stages of the evolution of parenthood adults were unable to view the child as a separate person from themselves. Parents projected on their children all the evil impulses, superstitions, hostilities, and sexual perversions of which they were possessed. Indeed, de Mause contends that generations of mothers and fathers impassively watched their infants and children suffer from one source of discomfort or another because they lacked the psychic mechanism necessary to empathize with children. The result he charges is that adults have committed a series of atrocities against children. The child in the past de Mause holds was so charged with projection that children were viewed as changelings "on the verge of turning into totally evil beings" (1974, 11). This belief that children could turn into monsters was one of the reasons why they were tied up, swaddled, and terrorized. De Mause catalogues the threatening figures and images which adults used to terrorize children into submission. "This need to personify punitive figures was powerful," de Mause observed, "adults actually dressed Katchina—like dummies to use in frightening children" (1974, 12).

De Mause and other historians cite evidence which indicates that infanticide was a regular practice in ancient civilizations and was not unheard of in Europe as late as the seventeenth and eighteenth centuries. Infanticide—the deliberate killing of infants—de Mause argues was a regular practice in the past. Among the Greeks as late as Aristotle's time there were no moral or legal restraints against the practice of infanticide. The Spartans inspected all free born children at birth deciding who would be allowed to live. Those who failed inspection were abandoned in the dung pit. (Sommerville, 1990, 20). Ancient Roman children "whose natural parents were unwilling or unable to raise them be exposed either to die or to be claimed by their finder" (Rawson, 1986, 172).

As de Mause traces the different modes of treatment meted out to children in the West he documents widespread infanticide in antiquity. In the past any child that was not perfect in shape and size, or cried too much, or was not physically normal was routinely put to death. Children were "thrown into rivers, flung into dung heaps and cess trenches 'potted' in jars to starve to death, and exposed on every hill roadside"(1974, 29). De Mause quotes a priest in 1527 who said that "the latrines resound with the cries of children who have been plunged into them" (1974, 29). Even legitimate children were deposited in the still of the night at the door of some charitable institution. Such abandonment was tantamount to infanticide.

Infanticide, rather than contraception or abortion, de Mause holds was the main method of controlling family size. The practice resulted in an unequal sex ratio. Throughout history, boys were valued much more than girls. De Mause notes that the few statistics available from antiquity show large surpluses of boys over girls: for instance, in 79 families who gained Milesian citizenship in 220 B.C. there were 118 sons and 28 daughters (1974, 26). De Mause insinuates that more girls than boys were put to death at birth.

The historian C. John Sommerville notes that in Carthage, child sacrifice was practiced. Children were sealed up in buildings to placate the gods. Archaeologists have dug into mass graves yielding the charred bones of thousands of children dated at about four years of age or younger (Sommerville, 47). The children who were sacrificed had lived long enough for their parents to have bonded with them. The welfare of the nation was felt to depend upon the sacrifice of children to the society's deities.

Rates of abandonment were also high. John Boswell's panoramic study (1988) of the abandonment of children from late antiquity to the Renaissance reveals how widespread the practice was among parents of all social classes. Boswell observes that early Christian moralists had only a few concerns about abandonment, and these involved incest rather than parental dereliction of duty. Boswell noted that while collecting information about early Christian mores he came across the argument by several theologians that men should not visit brothels or prostitutes because in doing so they might commit incest with a child that they had abandoned.

Rates of abandonment in Europe were high varying from 10%-25% in the eighteenth century. "Thus in the late eighteenth century in Toulouse," Boswell notes, "one child in four was known to have been abandoned." Rousseau wrote in his Confessions that:

> My third child was thus deposited in a foundling home just like the first two, and I did the same with the two following. I have five in all. This arrangement seemed to me so good, so sensible, so appropriate, that if I did not boast of it publicly it was solely out of regard for their mother…In a word, I made no secret of the action…because in fact I saw no wrong in it. All things considered, I chose what was best for my children, what I thought best…(1964, 424).

Rousseau was not desperately poor. However, he abandoned all five of his children to foundling homes, not even bothering to keep a record of their birth dates.

In traditional society, de Mause and other scholars argue that not only did mothers not love their children, but that their actions were deleterious and hurtful to their children. One harmful consequence of parental indifference was the pattern of sending children to wet nurses. Lacking an articulate sense of maternal love moved by material circumstance parents subordinated children's welfare to other objectives, such as keeping the farm going. One of the features of traditional European society was the large number of mothers who sent their small children away to be cared for by mercenary wet   nurses. The wet nurses drawn from agricultural laborers were poor harried women who generally lived in rural hovels. Evidence suggests that infants sent to wet nurses died at higher rates than those who remained in their own homes:

> Whereas the normal mortality of legitimate infants who stayed with their mothers was 19% in eighteenth-century Rounen, that of legitimate infants sent to rural wet nurses was 38 percent…In the city of Erfurt around 1870, 17 percent of all infants nursed by their own mothers perished before age one: 30 percent of those confined to wet nurses did so. It is thus clear that giving a child to a mercenary nurse appreciably increased the chances that its parents would never see it a gain (Shorter, 1977, 181).

The practice of using wet nurses was apparently denounced by physicians and moralists from the time of the ancient Greeks and the Romans, but the hold of custom was great. Even though it was generally known that infants died at higher rates when taken care of by wet nurses, parents continued to send them to what de Mause called "avenging goddess who required yet another sacrifice" (1974, 26).

If maternal breastfeeding made the difference between life and death then mothers did not pass what Shorter calls "the sacrifice test." To the extent that the breastfeeding was seen to interfere with sleep, that it would impair the shape of their breasts and their sexual attractiveness, and was perceived as a nuisance, they were putting their own well being ahead of their children. To the extent that they were willing to abandon wet nurses and breastfeed their children they were putting the welfare of their infants ahead of their attractiveness and convenience.

Children were also swaddled to prevent them from moving and were toilet trained to prevent inconvenience to adults. Restraints were thought necessary because the child was so full of "dangerous adult projections." The most significant result of swaddling was that it prevented the mother or wet-nurse from cuddling, hugging and caressing the child. And the convenience to adults was enormous. Once bundled up, infants rarely had to be supervised. The insides of children's bodies, de Mause contends, were also regulated. "Children were given suppositories, enemas, and oral purges in sickness and health," to break the will of the child so that parents could control the lives of children (1974, 39).

"The evidence which I have collected on methods of disciplining children," notes de Mause, "leads me to believe that a very large percentage of the children prior to the eighteenth century were what would today be termed 'battered children'" (1974, 40). Beating instruments included whips cat o nine-tails, shovels, and rods, and sticks. De Mause indicates the frequency of punishment by such examples as the German school teacher "who reckoned he had given 911,527 strokes with the stick, 124,000 lashes with the whip, 136,715 slaps with the hand, and 1,115,800 boxes on the ear" (1974, 41). Even noted humanists used severe means to control children. Milton's wife complained that the cries of his nephews distracted her. Beethoven whipped his pupils with a knitting needle and sometimes bit them (1974, 42). Urges to mutilate, burn, freeze, shake and throw infants violently "were continuously acted upon" (1974, 23). "In early modern times," de Mause noted, "the string underneath the newborn's tongue was usually cut, often with the midwife's fingernail, a sort of miniature circumcision."

Growing up in antiquity often involved sexual abuse. Growing up in the past often involved being used sexually by older men. The sexual use of children de Mause claims, "was everywhere evident in some form" (1974, 43). Boy brothels flourished in many cities. Children were frequently sold into concubinage. The sexual abuse by "pedagogues and teachers of smaller children" were common throughout antiquity. Literature and art de Mause pointed out confirmed cases of the sexual abuse of children. Petronius for example, depicted adults feeling the "immature little tool" of boys and described the rape of a seven year old girl with women clapping around the bed (1974, 45).

Explanations for the Emergence of Childhood

As the historians examined in this chapter are not in total agreement on all the important facts about the status of childhood in the past, they also disagree on the factors which were significant in bringing about the transformation of childhood. Explanations of the emergence of the modern notion of childhood have varied considerably.

Aries holds that the new sensitivity toward children can be found in a "revolution in feeling" toward the loss of a child which came to be defined as an overwhelming tragedy. Aries cites two reasons for the emergence of the modern notion of childhood. The main reason for this change Aries contends was a "demographic revolution." Drawing on demographic evidence, he argues that high infant mortality rates in the past deadened parental sensibilities toward their children, leaving their children vulnerable. He suggests that in a period of high mortality parents protected themselves against the emotional pain of a child's death by remaining emotionally aloof from the child. It was not rational to emotionally invest in a child "whose survival was problematical." Thus Aries notes Montaigne's observation that he had lost two or three children in their infancy, not without regret, but also without great sorrow (1962, 39) This indifference, Aries holds, was a direct consequence of the demographic conditions of the period.

From this perspective it would be unrealistic to invest too much emotional capital in such ephemeral beings. "People could not allow themselves," Aries held, "to become too attached to something that was regarded as a probable loss" (1962, 38). Such "demographic wastage" was countenanced because "people could not allow themselves to become too attached to something that was regarded as a probable loss" (1962, 38). For a child oriented society to develop it was essential that children should be less liable to sudden and early death than they were in the Middle Ages. To use the language of economists, the values of children rose as their durability improved, even if at the same time their maintenance costs rose. The decline in early mortality, therefore can be seen as an independent variable that encouraged the deepening of emotional bonds between parents and their children.

Aries also linked changes in the family with the shift in children's value. In *Centuries of Childhood*, he argues that the "discovery" of childhood as a separate stage of life in the sixteenth and seventeenth centuries in Europe, was a measure of the growing importance of family life: "The concept of the family...is inseparable from the concept of childhood. The interest taken in childhood...is only one form, one particular expression of this more general concept—that of the family." As instrumental ties weakened, the emotional value of all family members— including children—gained a new saliency.

C. John Sommerville argues that the increasing influence of Christianity also played a significant role, bringing about a decisive change in attitudes toward children. Sommerville has elaborated how Christianity was particularly significant in "sentimentalizing the image of the child" (1990, 55) Sommerville connects the change to Jesus' own statements about children and the attitudes these statements encouraged. The clearest statement on children was occasioned by an argument over who would be the greatest in the coming Kingdom. Jesus stated:

> Truly, I say to you, unless you turn and become like children, you will never enter the kingdom of God. Whoever humbles himself like this child, he is the greatest in the kingdom of God. Whoever receives one such child in my name receives me (Sommerville, 1990, 51).

Sommerville contends that such Christian religious understanding apotheosized the innocence and uncontaminated understanding of children. Jesus used children as a symbol of a saving trust and a new tenderness. Further it was insinuated that a good life could extend to the caring and nurturance of children

De Mause's interpretation of the transformation of childhood is psychologically oriented. De Mause argues for a psychoanalytic reading of childhood history and attempts to analyze the psychological principles that have characterized child/adult relations. In the past, he argues, parents were unable to view the child as a person separate from themselves, projecting on their children all the evil impulses, superstitions, hostilities, and sexual perversion of they were possessed because they lacked the psychic mechanism necessary to empathize with their children. He constructs a psychogenic model in which he depicts the adult in terms of three historical reactions 1) projective—the adults uses the child as a vehicles for the contents of their own unconscious 2) reversal—adults use the child as a substitute for adult figures important in their own childhood 3) empathic reaction—the adult can empathize with the child's needs and act to satisfy them.

It is, de Mause argues, the psychological transformation of the mentality of adults which accounts for the modern emergence of childhood. Through a process of "psychogenic evolution" adults "began to develop the capacity to identify and satisfy the needs of their children" (1974, 51). In this "psychogenic theory of history" de Mause interprets the evolution of parent-child relations as "an independent source of historical change, producing a generational pressure for psychic change in specific epochs."

De Mause periodizes the evolutionary development in which parents overcome their anxieties about their children and develop an empathic view into six stages:

1. The Infanticidal Mode (Antiquity to Fourth Century A.D.)
2. Abandonment Mode (Fourth to Thirteenth Centuries)
3. Ambivalent Mode (Fourteenth to Seventeenth Centuries)
4. Intrusive Mode   (Eighteenth Century)
5. Socialization Mode (Nineteenth to Mid-twentieth Centuries)
6. Helping Mode (Begins Mid-twentieth Century) (1974, 51-52)

Thus, the ultimate source of each new modal historical personality was not religious or demographic, but the psychic interaction between generations which produced generational patterns and personality types. It is emotion which moves history not demographics or economics. Humanity was less homo economicus than homo releatens.

Research on the transformation of childhood had been dominated by psychologists, historians, and demographers. Neil Postman, who calls himself a "media ecologist" provides a very different explanation for the transformation of childhood from an object of indifference to an object of sentiment. Postman focuses on the communication conditions that made childhood possible. In his examination Postman contends that the media of communication affected the socialization process; that it was the printing press that was the variable which created the modern status of childhood.

In his description of the status of childhood in the past Postman to a large degree recapitulates Aries' description of social indifference to children. Among the Greeks he finds no language to describe childhood and no children in their surviving statues. But rather than a complete absence of childhood he finds social and institutional traces of childhood. Herodotus, Postman notes, tells several stories that reveal an attitude toward childhood "recognizable to the modern mind" (1982, 6). Although the Greeks may have been confused about the nature of childhood they were passionate about education. They elevated education into a way of life. This was a new idea in human history, and it meant a new view of childhood. Postman credits the Greeks for "inventing" the school and establishing a great variety of schools. Thus, the Greeks move towards the recognition of the specialness of childhood because "wherever there are schools, there is consciousness, in some degree, of the specialness of the young" (1982, 7) Education implied that childhood would be marked as special period separate from the world of adulthood and for preparation for the world of adulthood. The result was that the Greeks gave the modern world a "foreshadowing of the idea of childhood" (1982, 8).

The Romans borrowed the Greek idea of childhood and built upon it, developing an awareness of childhood that surpassed the Greek idea of childhood. However the Romans made a connection between the child and shame. Postman argues this was immensely significant: "This was a crucial step in the evolution of the idea of childhood,... The point is simply, that *without a well-developed sense of shame, childhood cannot exist.*" (1982, 9). (Italics Postman) Postman holds that one of the main differences between the adult and the child is that the adult knows about certain facets of life that are not considered suitable for the child to know. Thus, the Romans began to conceptualize childhood by claiming for it the need to protect children from adult secrets. Social literacy expanded in Roman society resulting in the extension of the idea that children require protection and nurturing, and schooling, and freedom from adult secrets.

However, after the Roman period social literacy declined and so did childhood. It is, Postman believes, the decline of oralism and the development of the printing press and the subsequent rise of reading which ultimately establishes a separation of childhood from adulthood:

> Because reading makes it possible to enter a non-observed and abstract world of knowledge, it creates a split between those who cannot read and those who can. Reading is the scourge of childhood because, in a sense, it creates adulthood...Thus, in a literate world to be an adult implies having access to cultural secrets codified in unnatural symbols. In a literate world children must become adults (1982, 13).

In a non literate world there is no need to distinguish between the child and the adult for there are no secrets.

For Postman (1982, 18) the absence of literacy, the absence of educational institutions, and the absence of shame explain why the idea of childhood did not exist or take root in the ancient past; "It is the new communications environment which makes childhood possible: The printing press created a new definition of adulthood based on reading competence, correspondingly, a new conception of childhood based on reading incompetence." The printing press makes it necessary to become literate before having access to the secrets and the world of adults. Reading than in effect expels children from the world of adults and creates the necessity of childhood—a world for children to inhabit.

Since the emergence of childhood as a unique social status in Western society the concept of childhood has been a central term in theories, discussions, and research which have sought to understand the meaning of childhood in Western society. The work of Philippe Aries and much of the subsequent work inspired by Aries, is founded on the important assumption that much can be learned about a culture or a society by investigating the way it regards its children. The following chapter will examine the way social theorists have used the image of the child to understand society. In many works of social theory the child is not only historically important, but ideologically significant.

CHAPTER TWO
The Symbol of the
Child in Modern Social Thought

R. H. Tawney (1926, 268) observed that there is no touchstone which reveals the true character of a social theory more clearly than "its treatment of children." Tawney expresses an idea that became more or less inevitable with the emergence of the modern consciousness of childhood; that childhood was not only socially important, but ideologically significant; that the way in which a social theory represents or does not represent childhood is indicative of its own vitality, and worthy of scrutiny. This chapter seeks to explore the ideological status and meaning of childhood, as well as the ambiguous imagery that surrounds the consciousness of childhood in modern social thought.

One of the most influential works in the history of childhood is Philippe Aries' *Centuries of Childhood*. In this pioneering study Aries challenged the traditional assumptions about the changelessness of childhood, and argued instead that the idea of childhood had not even existed before the sixteenth or seventeenth centuries. Before this period, during the Medieval Era, Aries (1962, 128) held that "as soon as the child could live without the constant solicitude of his mother, his nanny or his cradle-rocker, he belonged to adult society." Aries attempted to show how historically recent in Western thought are our now dominant concepts of what childhood is. His basic thesis that childhood was a social category, and subject to historical processes has had an immense impact on the modern understanding of childhood.

It is an interesting historical paradox, that childhood once unknown, has now become the most analyzed phase in man's developmental cycle. Research on the status and value of childhood has been dominated by social historians, psychologists, and demographers. Historians (Aries 1962; de Mause 1974) have produced within the past two decades numerous works on childhood history and the social status of childhood, whereas very few were written prior to 1960. The plethora of psychoanalytic, cognitive, and behavioral models (Erickson 1950; Kohlberg 1973) of development attest to the attention and energy that has been brought to bear upon the life phase of childhood. Recently, a number of authors (Elkind 1981; Postman 1984; Winn 1983; Suransky 1985; Zelizer 1985) have examined the status of contemporary childhood. Yet, despite the vast amount of attention given to the historical status of childhood, the contemporary social status of children, and the psychological and cognitive development of children, little has been done to examine the ideological status of childhood in social theory; little attention has been paid to the "world view" that conveys an attitude toward everything about childhood from the trivial to profound in modern social thought. As Erik Erikson (1950, 16) critically observed in *Childhood and Society*, "One may scan work after work on history, society, and morality and find little reference to the fact that all people start as children and that all peoples begin in their nurseries."

Among the currents of scholarly inquiry there has been growing interest in the study of childhood.[1] The question inevitably arises, where are the children in sociological thought? When studied at all, their lives and experiences have been ghettoized in a few sociological sub-fields—the family, education, and socialization. Few of the students of social organization, work, political sociology, urban sociology, or even stratification pay close attention to the lives of children or the qualities of childhood. Sociological theory in particular is deeply adult centered, considering children mostly under the question of how the social order is reproduced.

The work of Aries, and much of the subsequent work inspired by Aries, is founded on the important assumption that much can be learned about a culture by investigating the way it regards its young. This chapter will deal with another form of the study of childhood—related, and yet significantly different in purpose and method. This chapter will focus on how social thought regards childhood. It is an effort to find underlying attitudes toward childhood in contemporary social thought in the hope of throwing some light, not only on the meaning of childhood in social thought, but on the way that the concept of childhood is joined to politics. It argues that theorists often use an image of childhood to uncover, define, or impose political meanings. This analysis is an attempt to retrieve from primarily modern twentieth century structures of consciousness the status of childhood, through an exploration of the ontogenetic assumptions and the imagery that surround the idea of childhood. It attempts to explore how the use and manipulation of these images not only defines and illuminates the nature of childhood and what children mean in society but is a vehicle and rhetorical strategy for the articulation of an analysis of society, an assessment of social change, and a vision of a utopian community.

The child has been a protean figure in Western thought (Kuhn, 1982). So ubiquitous and symbolic a figure is not a reproduction of a fact of existence, but a product of the imagination. That the various references and explications of childhood carry ideological commitments alongside their analytical components is understandable when we recognize that such models are constructed by theorists, not given by empirical situations.

In the parade of ideas in the history of social thought, concepts seldom march alone. Theorists have understood and identified both by pointing and distinguishing. Polarities, dualities and oppositional terms are abundant in the social sciences. The corpus of classical sociological work is filled with typologies: caste and class; rural and urban; primary and secondary; traditional and rational authority; substructure and superstructure. The concept of childhood can also be understood as one side of a significant and meaningful contrast.

The concepts of childhood and adulthood have been central terms in the discussions, research, and theories in which social theorists have tried to understand not only the meaning of childhood in society but to understand the present, compare it with the past, and imagine and understand the future. The opposition of these terms has sustained a dialogue both political and philosophical in its significance. It is the assertion of this inquiry that these two concepts are used not only to describe human development, but also act as metaphorical images of virtuous or vicious aspects of social life, including social change. They depict ideals to be sought and evils to be avoided. Of necessity, one concept cannot be discussed in the complete absence of the other. They exist in a kind of symbiosis, each revealing the meaning of the other. However, as childhood is the central reference in discussions of the meaning of childhood in society, the nature of social change, and the status of modern society, it will be the central focus of this inquiry.

In a world that includes children and childhood two views suggest themselves.[2] One view looks at growing up as form of acculturation, the process of giving up one culture for another, the way a native tribe takes on the culture of the West: the wild children give up their individualistic mores and join the tribe of society. The child is a "tabula rasa" who must be socialized and cultured. It follows that society can adapt children to anything if it uses the right techniques. Another view rejects adult models and affirms the natural virtue and wisdom of children unspoiled by repressive institutions. It considers children to be incomplete beings who in their very lack of completion possess gifts that are lost in the finished product of adulthood. They are "specula naturae," the mirrors of nature. The child is seen as the bearer of tremendously significant tidings.

In this chapter I make this distinction by using the terms modernist and anti-modernist to describe ideological camps with distinctive visions of childhood, politics, and society. In each camp there is an affinity between ideas of childhood and themes in social theory. The terms modernist and anti-modernist are clumsy and cumbersome. Unhappily they evoke the cultural polemics over "modernism" and "postmodernism" (Lears 1981; Bell 1978; Singal 1987). The terms are not used here to describe such cultural perspectives, nor are they used as a mechanism for pigeonholing. They are used here to describe broad intellectual currents that either affirm or oppose technological advancement. They identify general perspectives toward modern society, rather than positions on specific issues. The use of these terms here is intended to identify in as neutral language as possible the dichotomy between supporters and opponents of technological progress.

Many social theorists conceptualize an antagonism between society and childhood which takes the form of a metaphor of two worlds, a world of adulthood and a world of childhood in which the conflict is resolved only by renouncing either one or the other. There is an ideological conflict between what Ernst Schachtel (1959, 287–89) termed "childhood amnesia"—an inability to recover, and an unwillingness to value the worth of, childhood experience and memory; and the potential to recover "the riches of childhood experience." Technological enthusiasts view childhood as a threat to rationality and progress. Modernists, committed to the idea of progress and the promise of technology, find the experiences of childhood to be unacceptable and unusable in the modern world. For them the innocence of children is more a matter of the weakness of the limbs than of purity of the heart. In negative assessments of technological society, childhood is connected to an ancient Eden of innocence, and adulthood is equated with a doomed modernity lusting for science and power. Anti-modernists, critical of the notion of progress and suspicious of technology, provide a conceptualization in which childhood is linked to the possibility of a trans-schematic experience which widens the scope of human endeavor and human life. These two camps, with sharply conflicting views of childhood, have struggled to impose their definition of children's proper place in society; and have used the image of the child to dramatize and articulate different perspectives on society, progress, and social change.

Modernism and the Idea of Childhood

Modernist theorists embrace the great narrative of scientific, technological, and cultural progress. In their vision, science and technology have assumed a panacea-like character: given only time, all problems will capitulate to the emerging industrial order. Based on the premise that maturity is necessary and desirable, modernist thought frequently conceptualizes an antagonism between societal progress and childhood that is resolved in renouncing childhood. Modern prophets of progress accord childhood an inferior stature. They hold that the experience of childhood and the personality structure of childhood is incompatible with modern culture; that it becomes necessary in modern society that the remembrance of a time in which the potentialities of a fuller, freer and more spontaneous life were strongly present, be subordinated, if not extinguished entirely. Childhood is viewed as pleasurable, but inessential. In adult life it is deemed insignificant and thus trivialized.

Communities, classes, and individuals who do not fit the official technological mold tend to be viewed as "children," as incomplete beings who have yet to reach the age of maturity. The past is seen and judged in terms of development. In the words of Ortega y Gasset (1941, 217) "man has no nature, he has only his history." Ontological development is viewed as being analogous to historical development. Ontology is judged in terms of cumulative progressive development. Thus, in the modernist perspective, no condition prior to maturity is desirable.

To understand the full significance of childlike mentalities to modernist thinkers, we need first to glance at their imagery of childhood. Among those writers who express a modernist impulse, there is a common strand of developmentalism that is especially made clear in numerous pejorative references to "childishness" and "infantilism." The terms occur frequently enough to constitute a leitmotif in modernist discussions of society.

Post-industrial theorists have frequently accused their critics of being childish. Erich Fromm joined "the revolution of hope" against a resolutely cynical anti-technological movement. Fromm (1974, 156) belittled the "infantile fixation" of pastoral visions, urging instead a new social responsibility in which "intellect and affect are blended." Zbigniew Brzezinski (1976, 227–28) attacked the "ideological infantilism" of countercultural critics of industrial society. W.W. Rostow's (1960, 7) statement that events in eighteenth century England marked "the great watershed in the life of modern societies," which "on having occurred, was irreversible, like the loss of innocence," has become axiomatic in the work of modernization theorists. Victor Ferkiss (1970, 217) wrote that "Controlling technology in all its ramifications may be the supreme test of our species adulthood." In Ferkiss' *Technological Man*, the modern, popular attitude, so widespread in the United States that childhood is "sissy" is complemented by a notion that it is dysfunctional—that its promise of happiness and pleasure is a threat to the kind of activity, planning, and purposeful thought and behavior that is encouraged by advanced technological civilization. Arthur Schlesinger (1962, 254) put the case against childhood utopians cogently. "We must grow up now and forsake the millennial dream," he lectured those who he felt persisted in playing in the sandbox of life. This rhetorical strategy allowed modernists to portray themselves as "realistic" and mature at the expense of their opponents on the left, who were infantile and childish. Childhood is conceived as but the prelude to the serious business of life.[3]

For modernist theorists growth must lead to something new and better. Some explicitly argue a "recapitulation" model contending that the stages of human life are literally reproduced in the stages of societal development. The growth of society follows a natural pattern. It is irreversible. Kenneth Boulding (1964, 23-24) makes this argument without much subtlety:

> We cannot go back to the childhood of our race any more than we can go back to our own childhood without disaster. Eden has been lost to us forever and an angel with a flaming sword stands guard at its gates. Therefore either we must wander hopelessly in the world or we must press forward to Zion. (emphasis mine)

The historical past, like the individual past, is seen as a trap from which men must extricate themselves. Modernist theorists welcome the advent of "maturity" because of its use as a rational, pragmatic approach to the problems of life. Traditions are irrational reminders of the childhood of mankind. The world of technological civilization has no use for their kind of experience. Only those men who are free from the restraints of tradition, myth, and childlikeness, and who are capable of dealing with life in the most pragmatic terms can be regarded as truly mature and fit for full adult citizenship in modern technological society. Works of modernist sociology, anthropology, and psychology consistently use pejorative images and metaphors of childhood, denigrate childlike mentalities, and identify an antagonism between Western society and childhood.

Perhaps nowhere are these patterns more explicit than in the work of Talcott Parsons. Parsonian sociology, drawing on Freud, sees the individual in harmony with the repressive culture, and describes the process by which individuals play out their roles in society. No greater change in the needs of the individual occurs, Parsons maintains, than that which takes place between early childhood and adulthood. Into this change have gone all the decisive formative influences of the culture transmitted by the parents. From Parsons (1964, 203) point of view, "the process of transcending childhood" needs is at the same time the process of internalizing "higher levels of value." The first step here is the internalization of what Freud called the superego, which is the level of internalized control that makes the renunciation of childhood sexuality possible. The progressive repression of childhood sexuality, and the forgetfulness of this universally shared condition, is seen by Parsons as a means for the advancement of civilization.

In Parsonian theory the effective socialization of individuals seems highly predetermined. Through a series of stages a conception of the human condition is produced in which the individual is committed to maximal effort in the interest of achievement valued in the social system. "Every major step in achieving greater maturity," Parsons (1965, 203) holds, "involves the internalization of still higher levels of value commitment, up to the level of adulthood." Socialization mitigates the reinforcement of childlike responses. Socialization mechanisms, Parsons (1964, 212) declares, motivate the child "to conformity and dissuade him from deviance" from social expectations. Consequently, in "growing up" socialization encourages "high levels of discipline and responsibility." To the child "therefore, the most important goal to which he can orient himself is a contribution to the whole society" (Parsons 1965, 160). It is chiefly during the period of early childhood that the quality of the world changes for the growing child from a place where everything is to be explored to a place where everything is explained. In Parsons description of society the young, unable to discover enough friction even to begin to dream of rebellion, end up integrated to a world of adult values which are not to be questioned.

In addition to education, the extent of social differentiation in industrialized countries makes for greater differentiation between the position of adults and the position of children. "The greater responsibility of the adult in all societies, as compared with the child," Parsons (1964, 225) contends, "means above all that the capacity for inhibition, hence for affectively neutral orientations, for achievement must be developed to some important degree." There is no presumption of autonomy in Parsons view. The individual reproduces perfectly those roles assigned to him by society. Measured by such an emphasis on useful, efficient production and work norms, childhood becomes quite useless. The scheme of adult behavior, for Parsons, does not allow for childhood experiences or childlike perceptions of reality. Therefore it is not important to preserve those experiences or enable their recall. Childhood is a period of probation, unenviable from the vantage point of adulthood. Emancipation from childhood is a prerequisite of adulthood. In the Parsonian schema the child is not the father of the man, but dysfunctional to the man. The functional capacity of consciousness is limited to those types of experience which the adult consciously makes and is capable of making.

It was Talcott Parsons who first compared the doctor's role in psychotherapy to the parent's role in child rearing, suggesting certain similarities between mental illness and the child's family status. The child, Parsons (1959, 265) argued, cannot function in adult society independently, just as the mentally ill person cannot. The family provided a "broad situational framework within which the process of psychological adaptation and adjustment of individuals must take place." The success of psychotherapy sprung from the subterranean identification between the condition of childhood and the condition of mental illness. In the Parsonian scheme child rearing becomes a cure for the aberrant condition of childhood.

In Parsons' representation of childhood, formal continuity in time is offset by barrenness in content, by an incapacity to reproduce anything that resembles a really useful experience. Parsons pictures events as milestones rather than as moments filled with the unexplored wonders of life. In his (1964, 205) depiction of growing up, life is envisioned as a road with occasional signposts and milestones on the way pointing to "adjustment" and the "'normal functioning of the social system." The milestones are measurements of the "process of change in the state of the personality as a system" (1964, 204). Learning is a measure of the functional adjustments to the "interaction system;" so many years spent filling roles, so many years developing the "basic personality structure." For Parsons, modern western civilization, with its streamlined efficiency, uniform mass culture, and emphasis on usefulness in terms of profitable, material production is particularly and strikingly at the opposite pole from the world of childhood.

In *The Primitive World and Its Transformation*, a book which addresses the problem of cultural relativism and ethical neutrality, anthropologist Robert Redfield made much the same point about historical development. In Redfield's reading of history, humankind in the era of civilization had become adult because it had abandoned the childish ignorance and cruelty of pre-civilized life. "On the whole the human race has come to develop a more decent and humane measure of goodness," Redfield (1953, 163) observed, and in this sense "there has been a transformation of ethical judgment which makes us look at non civilized people, not as equals, but as people on a different level of experience. *I find it impossible to regret that the human race has tended to grow up.*" (emphasis mine) Redfield makes an analogy between primitive peoples and children in which each is found developmentally and culturally wanting. Redfield did not hesitate to adhere to such a doctrine of progress. To the argument that he (1953, 165) was ethnocentric and had violated his commission of objectivity he replied that "somehow the broken pledge—if it is broken—sits lightly on my conscience."

In the same vein that Parson's describes the social inferiority of childhood, and Redfield the cultural inadequacy of childlike underdevelopment, Jean Piaget, Bruno

Bettelheim, Erik Erikson and Freud describe the inferiority of the child's cognitive abilities. Although much of Piaget's work, particularly his experiments, recognizes the ingenuity, qualitative thinking, and curiosity of children, much of his theoretical and historical work tends to emphasize the developmental cognitive characteristics of children.

Piaget (1975, 74) argues that "since the intellectual prehistory of human societies may remain forever unknown to us, we must study the formation of these notions in the child, thus returning to a kind of mental embryology." He (1970, 13) attempts to explain how the transition is made "from a lower level of knowledge to a level that is judged to be higher." "It is with children," he (1970, 1) maintains, "that we have the best chance of studying the development of logical knowledge, mathematical knowledge, and so forth." The logical structures in the people can be explained through the understanding of the development of logical structures in children. In his observational work with children Piaget describes how children see the world differently from adults and restructure their experience accordingly.

Piaget (1975, 13–14) argues that the roots of logical thought are not to be found in language, but "in the coordination of actions, which are the basis of reflective abstraction." He regards the development of intelligence as a process that ends in mastery of formal logical categories based on formalistic principles and the absence of contradiction. At some point there is a radical change in conceptual codes which makes the progression from the prerational stage of childhood to the intellectual stages of adulthood. In his examination of the mental operations of children he deduced four principal stages through which the organism passes on its way to maturity and mastery. As in Rostow's theory of growth, which Piaget's theory schematically resembles, there is a necessary progression from one stage to another in which the child attained a logical consistency in behavior, knowledge, and action. The child advances from intuition and egocentrism to intellectual groupings. This structuring of reality Piaget (1971, 213) asserts is anterior to the emergence of formal logic and to a cognitive organization that is necessary "for the elaboration of the universe."

Piaget's assimilation-adoption model of child development, presupposes the correspondence between the roles assigned to individuals by the structures and the functions of the ongoing society and the internal system of values and beliefs that become objectified in patterns of social action. Piaget makes an attempt to integrate biogenetic orientation with the interaction of the organism with the environment. His theory of stages in the sensory-motor and conceptual development of the child provides an apparently adaptive relationship between self and society. Adaptation is equated with the maturation process, and assimilation is reduced to the internalization of the structure of legitimate social life.

Piaget's theory does not grant much of a creative role to the thought of children, to the relationship of children to one another in play, friendship, or imagination. In Piaget's description of cognitive development, the capacity for immediate sensuous enjoyment is lacking. As Brian Sutton-Smith (1971, 332) notes:

...as undirected thinking, fantasy, play etc., are specifically childlike and mainly compensatory, that is having nothing to do with the development of particular kinds of intellectual operations, *they may be confined to the infantile stage and regarded as irrelevant to the nature of adult intellectual operations.*

(emphasis mine)

Childhood cognition is conceived as a period of backwardness, useless from the vantage point of adult cognition. Piaget deprives childhood of any constitutive role within thought; childhood can only repeat and replicate, it can never originate.

For Piaget the intellectual structure of adult cognitive functions does not contain categories within which the childhood world can be subsumed or experienced. It simply is incompatible with the experience of a previous age. While in an adult state, operating in an experiential realm that makes practical demand, man employs a linguistic system which is perfectly suitable for survival, but which does not enable, use, or cope with matter foreign to it, whether this material comes from the domain of childhood or that of dreams.

Starting from a logical and rational understanding of knowledge, Piaget's experimental research leads to an epistemological elaboration in which the man explains the child and the child is eliminated from the man. The child advances from a stage of infantile egocentrism that Piaget (1971, 216–17) pejoratively describes as "a type of ignorance of the inner life and a deformation of the self coupled to a misconception of objective relationships," to a stage of operational intelligence. Piaget makes the analogy that the laws of thought are identical to the laws of the world, of nature. His "genetic epistemology," very much like Darwin's survival of the fittest, translates the concepts of formalized reason into a natural history which regards cognition as a natural organ. "Genetic epistemology," like Darwinism, rejects any elements of the child's mind that transcend the function of adaptation and is not an instrument for self preservation. The child, then, for Piaget, is an undeveloped person an incomplete being. Society is in need of complete persons, not incomplete persons, in its quest to further understand the universe.

Like Piaget, Bruno Bettelheim is concerned with the mechanisms that facilitate growing up. Bettelheim argues that fairy tales bring about the adaptation of the child to reality. They help children to grow out of childhood. In *The Uses of Enchantment*, Bettelheim suggests that facing up to well entrenched fears as the child does when he bravely weathers the telling of a horrific fairy tale, has the effect—if properly managed—of dispelling fears and building self confidence. On their own, Bettelheim argues, children are not yet able to make sense of their internal processes. Fairy tales offer figures on to which the child can externalize what goes on in his mind in controllable ways that promote psychological maturation; they engender a sense of security in which the child no longer needs "to hold on to infantile projections," freeing him "to seek rational explanations" (Bettleheim, 1977, 51). The fairy tale, Bettleheim feels, offers fantasy materials which suggest to the child in symbolic form what the battle to achieve self realization—adulthood—is about. It helps the child master the psychological problems of growing up and relinquishing "childhood dependencies." It also illuminates the advantages of growing up. Significantly, the heroic figures of fairy tales are often the wisest, the biggest, and the oldest. Children need help in finding meaning in life—to become adults. "Only in adulthood," Bettelheim (1977, 3) asserts, "can intelligent understanding of the meaning of ones existence in the world be gained from ones experiences in it."

Erik Erikson also contends that the emotional residues of childhood inhibit emotional development. Noting that civilized cultures have a long childhood Erikson (1950, 16) observed that:

> Long childhood makes a technical and mental virtuoso out of man, but it also leaves a lifelong residue of emotional immaturity in him. While tribes and nations, in many intuitive ways, use child training to the end of gaining their particular form of mature human identity, their unique version of integrity, they are, and remain, beset by the irrational fears which stem from the very state of childhood which they exploited in their specific way.

In *Childhood and Society* Erikson traces the relationship between the anxieties of childhood and the crises of modern society. In several case studies he explores the problems of identity connected with the entry of America, Germany, and Russia into the industrial revolution. He argues that the immature origin of man's conscience endangers his works since infantile fear accompanies him through life, culminating in "adult destructiveness." Erikson (1950, 406) examines how "those fears, apprehensions, and urges which are derived from the arsenal of infantile anxiety" are projected on to political and economic life, causing social upheaval and social dislocation. Each generation he insinuates, must develop out of childhood in order to establish a just society. (And psychology must understand the "fateful function of childhood" in order to help bring adjust society about.)

It is Freud who did more than anyone else to demolish the myth of an innocent childhood paradise and to focus attention on the earliest stages of life as the crucial period in human development. Childish traits he deems as obstacles to the development of the mature adult, for the child is nothing more than a homonuculus, a primitive form of the complex and higher being represented by man. In *The Interpretation of Dreams* Freud (1913, 107) states unambiguously that children are of interest only as underdeveloped subjects:

> The most simple dreams of all, I suppose are to be expected in the case of children, whose psychic activities are certainly less complicated than those of adults. The psychology of children, in my opinion, is to be called upon for services similar to those which the study of the anatomy and development of the lower animals renders to the investigation of the highest animals.

Rarely does Freud (1964, 76) go beyond insisting, as he does in *Leonardo da Vinci and a Memory of his Childhood*, that childhood is "not the blissful idyll into which we distort it in retrospect."

Freud offers a view of modernist thought in a microcosm. In his metahistory of psychological development Freud described three stages of social progress; the age of primal man, the age of religious civilization, and the dawning age of scientific civilization, the best of all possible if not all imaginable, worlds. In his description of historical development Freud could not resist the image of the child growing to personhood. In the age of religion, Freud (1964b, 81) insisted people had played the part of children, but in the nascent age of science and reason: "they will be in the same position as a child who has left the parental house where he was so warm and comfortable. *But surely infantalism is destined to be surmounted. Men cannot remain children forever.*"(emphasis mine)

At the ontogenetic and phylogenetic level Freud viewed childhood as a retreat from modernity. Freud, indeed, spoke of "the costs" of civilization and regarded neurosis as a part of the price man paid for civilization, but he never said that the price was too high to pay for civilization and he never meant that humans should abandon their civilized aims. Freud was sometimes disappointed in the development of civilization. But just as the individual must grow up, he observed, so must societies. Noting that religion was "comparable to a childhood neurosis," he (1964b, 81) optimistically held "that mankind will surmount this neurotic phase."

The preceding discussion of sociological, anthropological, and psychological images and conceptualizations of childhood indicates the degree to which the meaning of childhood is encapsulated in structures of consciousness that are characterized by a linear, rational epistemology of human and social development. These examples all attest in varying degrees to the impositional structures of consciousness that an ideological world of celebrants of progress have brought to bear upon the life phase of childhood. All that a child was, is, or could become, is observable and measurable against the standard of adulthood.

Anti-Modernism and the Idea of Childhood

There is an opposite interpretation of the concept of childhood. Anti-modernist theorists, recoiling from what they see as the over civilized state of modern existence, and celebrating more intense forms of physical and spiritual existence, exalt authentic experience as an end in itself. Their protest against a complacent faith in progress and a narrow, reductionist, and positivist conception of reality embraces childhood as an important symbol of an alternative to the sterility of twentieth century positivism and technology. Anti-modernist theorists urge that society affirm and accept childhood with all its potentialities. The childhood virtues of spontaneity, purity, and innocence must be nurtured and celebrated. Children are the center of hope. Anti-modernists thus seek to reconcile childhood and society, encouraging the reception and reproduction of experiences of early childhood.

This view makes children into a special class, not to control or mold them, but to conserve them as a natural resource or natural wonder. The key terms are not children's development or growth but their spontaneity, fantasy, animality, creativity, and innocence. Anti-modernists see childhood as the period of life that is richest in experience, for everything is new to the child; his gradual grasp of the environment and the world around him are experiential in scope and quality beyond any discoveries of adult life. Children contribute something besides their raw materials or muscle to man's heritage. They come up with original ways of viewing a world hardened, stratified, and over-weaned by its own power. Anti-modernists sense that modern life has grown dry and passionless, and that one must somehow try to regenerate a lost intensity of feeling. To this end they seek the recovery of childhood experience. This view is forcefully put forward by authors associated with critical theory, and more recently the counterculture.

Among the twentieth century thinkers who have pondered most carefully the fate of childhood in technological society are the critical theorists. One of the greatest costs of progress, critical theorists continually remind us, is the repression of memory—particularly childhood memory. "All reification," Theodore Adorno observed, "is forgetting: objects become thing-like at the moment when they are grasped without being fully present in all their parts, where something of them is forgotten" (Schroyer, 1975, 191). The totality and wholeness that technological societies denied, exist, and could be sought in childhood, since children had not yet sensed the irreversible and ineluctable impoverishment which leads to adulthood.

The hidden quality of lost childhood memories, their separation from the rest of life, their inaccessibility, and their incompatibility with conventional, purposeful, daily, activity are described lucidly by Walter Benjamin. Benjamin, himself a collector of children's books, appreciated the richness of experience to the child. Benjamin's writing on childhood attempted to capture those moments of wonder, encapsulated in the simple gesture, the single action of a very young child. Benjamin believed that the child's grasp of his environment and the world around him went far beyond any discovery made in adult life. "For children," Benjamin (1973, 102) wrote:

> ...can accomplish the renewal of existence in a hundred unfailing ways. Among children, collecting is only one process of renewal; other processes are the painting of objects, the cutting out of figures; the application of decals—the whole range of childlike modes of acquisition, from touching things to giving them names.

To Benjamin, no Columbus, no Marco Polo had ever seen stranger and more fascinating and thoroughly absorbing sights than the child who learning to perceive, to taste, to smell, to touch, to see and use their body experienced. Benjamin idealized the child's capacity for unrepressed emotional and imaginative experience. In childhood, he found the self to be not only vigorous, but whole. Benjamin saw children as the incarnation of a miracle that awoke the sense of the marvelous not only in themselves, but in those who encountered them.

In Benjamin, the anti-modern impulse leads towards an apotheosis of simplicity and a fascination with the enchanted, the uncanny, and the inexplicable. He (1973, 102) found these qualities in childhood and the fairy tales of childhood. He took fairy tales so literally that he suggested that they made real fulfillment possible—particularly to children.

> The wisest thing—so the fairy tale taught mankind in olden times, and teaches children to this day—is to meet the forces of the mythical world with cunning and with high spirits...The liberating magic which the fairy tale has at its disposal does not bring nature into play in a mythical way, but points to its complicity with liberated man. A mature man feels this complicity only occasionally, that is, when he is happy; but the child first meets it in fairy tales, and it makes him happy.

Whereas Bettelheim examined the uses of enchantment, Benjamin was drawn to the sense of enchantment; the engagement with "liberating magic" that the child experiences in the fairy tale. Benjamin depicted the child's sense of knowing and understanding as transformative. For it is these history-making acts of the child he felt which invests everyday life experiences with consciousness and meaning.

As early as 1941 Max Horkheimer expressed a serious concern with the disappearance of childhood. Just as the presence of the child could be a cause for joy, so its loss could be a tragedy. "Development has ceased to exist," Horkheimer (1941, 381) wrote:

> The child is grown up as soon as he can walk. During the heyday of the family the father represented the authority of society to the child, and puberty was the inevitable conflict between these two. Today, however, the child stands face to face with society at once, and the conflict is decided even before it arises.

Horkheimer regarded this as unfortunate. The separation that the adult world imposed between reality and play and the demarcation of these activities into specific contexts was not part of the normal structure of childhood. He believed children did not view the world like that—at least not until they were taught to do so. In his (1941, 381) striking phrase, "The child, not the father, stands for reality." But in the technological era, a space where children could be at home in the world, where they could be the subject and not only the object of history, no longer existed.

In *Eclipse of Reason* Horkheimer searched for a liberated future through regaining the "mimetic impulse of the child." Imitation, Horkheimer argued, was one of the primary means of learning in early childhood. The whole body was an organ of mimetic expression in which such manners as laughing, crying and speaking were acquired. Eventually, however, civilization transcended the mimetic impulse in favor of rational, goal directed behavior:

> Conscious adaptation and, eventually, domination replace the various forms of mimesis. The progress of science is the theoretical manifestation of this change: the formula supplants the image, the calculating machine the ritual dances. (1977, 115)

Horkheimer, however, implied that mimesis need not be repressed; it could imitate life-affirming characteristics such as the sense of justice of the father and the instinct-tual love of the mother that were superseded by later civilization. The imitative impulse, Horkheimer (1977, 179) argued, could be restored through language:

> Language reflects the longings of the oppressed and the plight of nature; it releases the mimetic impulse. The transformation of this impulse into the universal medium of language rather than into destructive action means that potentially nihilistic energies work for reconciliation…Philosophy helps man to allay his fears by helping language fulfill its genuine mimetic function, its mission of mirroring the natural tendencies. Philosophy is at one with art in reflecting passion through language and thus transferring it to the sphere of experience and memory.

Ontogenetically Horkheimer maintained that this condition is present in the young child, it is only later tragically overcome by civilization and maturity.

For Horkheimer the child lived in open communication with the world, and the world in turn invited exploration from the child. Speech for children was not only an instrument of communication, but the very essence of their jubilant nature. Things in the world challenged the child, disclosed themselves to the child. Language comprised the mode through which the child realized himself. It was through language that the child restructured, invented, made history and transformed his given reality, for the transforming nature of language allowed the child to become fully realized as a human being. It was vital, Horkheimer felt, that the child be permitted to live this life-phase fully, to play and let things disclose themselves.

For Horkheimer language was the child's praxis on the adult world—and man's hope for an alternative to the deterministic laws of technological society. As long as the adult can recover through the intellect, the imagination or the involuntary memory, the mental set of the child, and appropriate for himself the schemata within which the child orders the elements of his experiences, then he can relieve the profound reality of his erstwhile condition, and can even retranslate it into terms comprehensible to other adults.

This apotheosis of childhood is stated in compelling form by Ernst Block. A student of utopian thought, Block argued that history was not subject to deterministic laws that left no place for man and his dreaming. Block's (Wagar,1972,333) vision of history culminated in nostalgia for the "homeland" seen in childhood, and lost to adulthood:

> The root of history is working, creating man, man who transforms and outstrips the conditions of his existence. Let him achieve self-comprehension and ground his life in real democracy, without renunciation and estrangement; *then, something will arise in the world that all men see in childhood, a place where no one has yet lived; homeland.*(emphasis mine)

In the return to the lost world of childhood the love and security sacrificed by the catastrophe of growing up are recaptured. The more acute the suffering of the time of separation, the more keen the joy of returning home again.

The recovery of childhood is a prominent theme in the countercultural critique of modern technological life in the late 1950's and the 1960's. The distinction between "straight" and "hip" often divided generations. This notion was perhaps best epitomized in the Yippie slogan not to trust anyone over thirty. The association between the innocence of childhood and the romantic idea of childhood wisdom was explained by the fact that children had not yet had the opportunity to learn the terms by which an adult perspective is defined. One of the Movement's dominant themes entailed a devaluation of adulthood as a bad bargain with life in which one gave up more than one got. "I am never quite free of the forces attempting to make me grow up, sign contracts, get an agent, be a man," Raymond Mungo (1970, 136–37) observed in his memoir of the counterculture. "I have seen what happens to men. It is curious how helpless, pathetic, and cowardly is what adults call a Real Man...If that is manhood, no thank you."

Again and again countercultural authors exalt childhood and childlike characteristics. Many of the dissenting figures of counterculture in the sixties discovered in the child the harbinger and the shape of a cultural revolution. Norman O. Brown (1972, 60) urges man "to regain the lost laughter of infancy." In *Slaughter House Five*, subtitled "The Children's Crusade," Kurt Vonnegut's (1969) hero Billy Pilgrim is a childlike figure who invents himself and his universe as a way of coping with the harsh reality of World War II. Norman Mailer found the saving quality of the hipster-psychopath's behavior in the retreat to childhood. Mailer noted that when the psychopath acted out his infantile fantasies, he was trying to go back to the early days of his life, which had determined his character and course ever since, and remake the decisions that led inexorably to the present. In his attempt "to try to live the infantile fantasy" (Mailer, 1959, 320) the hipster-psychopath tries to reconnect with his childhood rather than trying to repress it. Theodore Roszak (1975, 114), who tried to capture the zeitgeist of the movement in his book *The Making of a Counterculture*, extolled his readers to recapture "our childish sense of the world enchanted." Instead of politicization as a means to perceptive self-consciousness and human emancipation he appealed to an increasing "adolescentation."

Though dissent during the sixties did not remain strictly theoretical, the period saw the reception of several authors whose works were deeply hostile to the dominant spirit of the age. Often, as noted above, they found alternative possibilities in the recovery of child-like forms of consciousness. Two theorists who rationalized this theme and gave it structure were Herbert Marcuse and Paul Goodman.

Herbert Marcuse attempts to redefine the social status of the child, transforming Original Sin into Original Innocence. Western society, Marcuse argues, has developed a concept of childhood which contains the dominant features of what he terms "the performance principle." However, Marcuse contends that childhood, along with art and phantasy contain the negation of "the performance principle." Childlike fantasy retains the structure and tendencies of the psyche prior to organization by reality. Thus, childhood links the deepest layers of the unconscious with the products of consciousness; preserving the archetypes of liberation, the tabooed images of freedom. Childhood preserves the meaning of the sub historical past; images of liberation are kept alive in literature, art, and in the imagination of children. "Historical possibility," Marcuse (1962, 145) contends, is present in "childish fantasy."

To Marcuse, freedom from social conventions and utilitarian calculation made the child an emblem of a fuller, more sensuous and imaginative life and a focal point for a potentially sharp critique of modern society. In Marcuse's work, childhood remembrance becomes a decisive weapon in the struggle against domination. Domination is made possible, he suggests, because the "ability to forget" sustains submissiveness and renunciation. Such forgetfulness reproduces the conditions that produce injustice and enslavement. "Against this surrender to time," he (1962, 212) continued, "the restoration of remembrance to its rights, as a vehicle of liberation, is one of the noblest tasks of thought." Childhood represents remembrance, and is viewed as a vehicle for the liberation from the restraints of civilization. For Marcuse the nature of childhood had two distinct but related social uses. On the one hand, an exaltation of childishness pointed to a critique of technological society. Childhood presented a new reality with an order of its own. Childhood also provided a mechanism for a brief imaginary escape from technological society.

Paul Goodman (1960, xvi) was among the first strong voices to say that the problem of growing up in American society derived from the nature of society rather than the deviance of young people. "I assume," Goodman wrote, "that the young really need a more worthwhile world in order to grow up in at all." In *Growing Up Absurd* he described how the system "thwarted and insulted" the natural qualities of youth. In his later thinking on the subject Goodman added to the traditional romantic view of childhood as innocence or noble savagery the argument that helping to preserve what is best in the natural wildness of children involves adults as children; that is, it calls upon adults to reach for residues of their own childhood from which they may have only reluctantly "come down" into maturity. Goodman (1977, 143) commended the retrospective creation of adults who have sought to become like unto children, who can "draw upon child powers without inhibition." As long as the adult could recover the mental set of the child as appropriate for himself, Goodman felt, then he could understand the profound reality of his condition.

Anti-modernists contrast the riches of childhood experience, the child's great capacity for impressions and experience, with of the poverty of mature adult perceptions of experience. They express a nostalgia for lost innocence—the possibility of continuing to be childlike and pure in an increasingly corrupt and aging world. The key to bliss is not science and learning, or any transcendence that man can store up in himself, but a childlike state of innocence. Modern man can only achieve happiness by finding the garden of childhood once more.

Conclusion

As the preceding discussion indicates the child is a protean figure in contemporary social theory. So ubiquitous and symbolic a figure is no mere reproduction of a fact of existence; he is a cultural and ideological invention, a product of the imagination—a product of ideological construction. But for what has he been invented? Within the dialogue of modern social theory, positions on the nature of childhood have been one way in which commitments have been marked in significant ideological disputes. This inquiry has sought to demonstrate that in the work of many leading modern social theorists, perspectives on childhood are connected with important issues in social theory.

This inquiry has attempted to show how the dichotomy of childhood and adulthood has been a major framework within the poles of which social theorists have set their discussions of major themes and issues. In the preceding discussion I have attempted to examine analyses of modern technological society as two ideological perspectives which hold distinctive assumptions about the ontology of childhood, that use distinctive images and metaphors of childhood, and connect the idea of childhood to assumptions about civilization, history, progress, time, and visions of a utopian community.

The differences between these two perspectives can be seen most vividly by attending to the contrasting ontology of childhood put forward. Modernists describe children as incomplete beings who are in some way deformed. They suffer from what Piaget called "a deformation of the self." Childishness and infantalism are viewed as constituting some kind of congenital infirmity which negates a rational, pragmatic approach to existence. On the other hand anti-modernists find a more intense and spiritual sense of experience in childhood. According to this view, children are primarily creatures who experience the world through their feelings (their "hearts"), unlike adults who operate through reason. Childhood, because it is untainted by social artifice, embodies the moral innocence and emotional spontaneity which appears to be absent in modern society. Historical possibility is held to be present in "childish fantasy." Children are perceived as incomplete beings who in their very lack of completion possess gifts that are lost in the finished product. Their essence is viewed as organic and natural, requiring only that it not be suffocated by civilization's diseased outpourings in order to flower.

Each perspective views the relationship of childhood to civilization quite distinctively. Anti-modernists view the child as a personage, born to, if not living in a state of nature, basically good until the forces of civilization corrupt their naive essence. They posit the existence of childhood within a state of benign nature whose vitality is gradually but inexorably sapped by the force of civilization. The child's innocence is dissipated in the world of duty and work. Not the proletariat, but the child is an innocent victim. A litany of loss permeates this camp and provides a center about which concerned voices cluster. The loss lamented by one camp is loudly cheered by the other. For the modernist, childhood is brought to goodness, and is redeemable, only through training designed to eliminate irrationality and spontaneity. Childhood is not an end in itself, but a preliminary. The gradual passage from childhood to adulthood is a normal and desirable progressional development.

Each perspective uses the image of childhood to understand the notion of progress. Where the anti-modernists bemoan the passage of childhood, the modernist finds the passage of childhood a welcome and sought-after transformation. The passage of childhood mentalities is even prescribed as a means of progress and a pre-condition for civilization. The nature of childhood development is reified into schemas which delineate the stages and patterns of childhood development. The linear evolutionary schema suggests that social change requires rationality and maturity. In the modernist view the child is an unformed person who, through socialization, education, reason and self-control, may be made into a civilized adult. For anti-modernists, Western civilization, with its emphasis on rationality and efficiency, is at the opposite pole from childhood.

In the anti-modernist view it is not the unformed child that is a problem, but the deformed adult—the adult who has lost his childlike sense of wonder. Growing up, is not an advance. Anti-modernists attempt to reconstitute the world of the child and use it as a framework for their own retrospective concerns. Many desire to recapture the essence of a lost past.

The child possesses as his or her birthright, capacities for candor, understanding, curiosity and spontaneity that are deadened by education, reason, self-control and imposed maturity. Freedom from social convention and utilitarian calculation makes the child an emblem of a fuller, more sensuous and imaginative life—a focal point for a sharp critique of industrial society.

These assessments of childhood also yield different perspectives on history and time. For the modernist theorist the world in which children live is one in which children are the objects, not the subjects of history. In the institutional world that infants and children confront—the family, the schools, the media--they are shaped, not shapers. Children reside in a world without directed intentionality. Their being is defined by others. Reality is constituted without praxis. History is made of them, not by them. Underdeveloped societies, as well as individuals are outside of history. The "loss of innocence," to use Rostow's phrase, is a necessary prerequisite to modernization. The nature of childhood evokes distrust. In modernist theory the concept of development provides a model for asserting that modern history, in contrast to traditional history, is predictable and progressive.

In childhood, anti-modernist theorists hold, people can step beyond existing arrangements and perceptions of history and freely create an alternative history and reality which projects what "can be." Childhood is viewed as the herald of a golden age. They emphasize the redemptive quality of childhood. They use the relationships experienced in childhood to stand in contradiction to the hierarchical and static features of established forms of social interaction. They want to recover what children know and adults have forgotten—such things as sensitive receptivity and utopian awareness. They see childhood as an organizing experience, which is free from both external and internal compulsions, is non-instrumental, and transcends the static idea of being and history.

For modernists time can be measured and is envisioned as a progressive seriation of events. Since the advent of the industrial revolution modernists have contemplated the promise of a more luxurious estate in which not only the prospect of maximum leisure and enjoyment, but human freedom and independence were dependent upon sustained scientific and technological advancement. In this perspective childhood and childishness is perceived as subversive to the development of rationality and the establishment of order. Anti-modernist theorists are well aware of the structural parallels between the suppression of childhood and the suppression of time. The quality of early childhood experience does not fit into the linear schemata of adult experience, thought, and memory. Time, that implacable enemy of childhood, must be suspended. The quality of early childhood experience is felt to transcend the repression of modern society, affirming instead the total personality with all its potentialities. Childhood leads both to a critique of the dominant culture and an effort to revitalize it. In the memories and experiences of childhood, lies the basis for a transcendence of the conventional schemata of history and time, for a widening of the scope of human time and human history. Human history is conceived not as a routine proceeding from one stage to another, driven by some clockwork mechanism, but as a process in perpetual transformation, filled not with a technological capacity fashioned by adult culture, with all its biases, emphases, and taboos, but by the child's struggle to unfold and become.

Within the dimensions of the childhood-adulthood dichotomy modern social theorists have also connected metaphorical images of childhood to utopian visions of community. Modernists express the notion that an originally corrupted nature must be trained into a semblance of orderly virtue. The adult has some chance of attaining goodness, the child none. Adulthood is the touchstone of morality. The contours of utopia are a mirror image of adulthood; rational, pragmatic, civilized, mature—grown up. Anti-modernists express the notion that falling short of adulthood is a guarantee of insight, innocence, and virtue. They find childhood to be a kind of latter-day pastoralism which finds a Golden Age not at the end of history, but at the beginning of each lifetime. They see in childhood the possibility for the fulfillment of their own dreams. Childhood is the touchstone for morality. The contours of utopia are a mirror of childhood; sensuous, spontaneous, innocent, and open. For both camps the concept of childhood has its ideological usage as a contrast between what is and what could be.

NOTES

1. The status of childhood has been systematically examined in several significant areas of scholarship. *In Pricing the Priceless Child: The Changing Social Value of Childhood* (1985) Vivian Zelizer traces the dramatic transition of children from an economically useful but emotionally disvalued being, to an economically "worthless" but emotionally "priceless" child in American society. Zelizer examines the changing attitudes toward the death of children, the status of child labor, children's insurance, compensation for wrongful death, and the adoption and sale of children. Zelizer argues that these changes were brought about by social factors,

primarily the expulsion of children from the cash nexus of labor at the turn of the century.

In *Corruption in Paradise: The Child in Western Literature*, (1982), Reinhold Kuhn examines the literary manifestation of the child in literature. Kuhn examines the context in which fictional children were discussed.

The changing "metaphorical and analogical" understanding of children is also discussed in the context of the historical evolution of developmental psychology in a symposium in the *American Psychologist* 1986, 1218-1230). The image of the child is examined in terms of the definition of what a child is, and what the child's cognitive abilities are.

2.   These notions are by no means limited to contemporary theory. The former view is associated with John Locke, the latter with Jean-Jacque Rousseau and the Romantic poets. John Locke argued that childhood could be understood as a state of underdevelopment, deficient in rationality, cognitive abilities, knowledge, and maturity. In his book *Some Thoughts Concerning Education*, Locke proposed an education that, while it treated the child as a precious resource, nonetheless demanded rigorous attention to children's intellectual development and capacity for self control. Even Locke's views on the nurturing of physical growth had as their purpose the development of a child's power of reason. A child must have a vigorous body, he (1922, 35) wrote, "so that it may be able to obey and execute the orders of the mind." Locke argued that without the development of reason, industry and virtue a child was "in danger (of) never being good for anything."

A second approach envisioned childhood as a state of innocence and wonder. This was how Jean-Jacques Rousseau used the idea of childhood. "Love childhood," wrote Rousseau (1964, 37) in *Emile,* "Indulge its games its pleasures and its lovable nature. Who has not looked back with regret on an age when laughter is always on the lip and when the spirit is always at peace. Why take away from these little innocents the pleasure of a time so short which ever escapes them." Rousseau (1964, 68) argued that childhood has "its own way of seeing, thinking, and feeling, and nothing is more foolish than to try to substitute ours for theirs."

3.   The theme also emerges in fictionalized form as well. In Henry Roth's novel *Call It Sleep*, which is considered by many critics to be the most distinguished of American "proletarian novels," technical progress and growing out of childhood are intriguingly linked. David Schearl, an immigrant child isolated by his childishness, the threatening existence of the streets, and the hostility of his father pushes a milk ladle through the crack in the street car tracks where the power line runs. He is jolted unconscious. He awakes with a more mature sense of experience. The power which convulses his body transforms him from an infant to a man. Roth uses the machine as a mystical force for personal transformation, insinuating its power for social transformation as well.

CHAPTER THREE

The Child In The Courtroom: Issues of Children in Court Proceedings

As child abuse, custody, and adoption cases involving children have come before the courts the presence of children as witnesses in the legal system has become a significant social issue. The last decade has seen an unprecedented concern, both in the United States and abroad, for the plight of abused children in the legal system (Spencer 1992; Nicholson and Murray 1992). Increasingly, children are appearing in court, prompted mainly, but not entirely by the growth in cases of alleged child sexual and physical abuse. According to Stephen Ceci and Maggie Bruck (1996) more that 200,000 children are currently involved in the legal system in a given year. Recently, upwards of 13,000 children, disproportionately of preschool age, have yearly been involved in testifying in sexual abuse trials. Because of the unique attributes of child witnesses—their cognitive and emotional maturity, their position as the most critical source of evidence in sexual abuse cases—their presence in judicial process has raised many controversies. This chapter examines the background of children in the legal system, the issues that their presence in the legal system has raised, and reforms in the legal system.

The History of Children in the Legal System

Few subjects evoke stronger emotions than children, victimization, abuse and or sex (Crewdson, 1988; Finkelhor, 1988). When these converge in child abuse cases the stage is set for the emergence of significant emotional and social issues. For years child abuse was believed to be rare in the United States and the subject was rarely discussed in the media or studied by academicians. Prior to 1962 academicians and journalists paid little attention to assaults by parents and others on children. Prior to 1962 those writing about social problems paid little attention to physical assaults on children (Best 1993). Family doctors often ignored cases of child abuse and failed to report it when they saw it (Pfohl, 1977). Violence against children had a long history (Pleck, 1987), but child abuse only became considered a significant social problem in the contemporary United States when claims were made that children were being seriously abused and others began to respond to those claims.[1]

The growth of public and professional concern about battered children occurred in the early 1960's. Attention was drawn to this problem by the medical profession, particularly radiologists and pediatricians, who reversed the previous lack of attention shown by doctors to the existence of abuse. The medical discovery of child abuse was initiated by pediatric radiologists studying the X-rays of children who had suffered fractures or blows to the skull. Thus radiological evidence cast doubt on the claim of a parent or guardian that a child had not been previously injured.[2]

When C. Henry Kempe published "The Battered Child Syndrome" in the *Journal of the American Medical Association* in 1962 this era of indifference came to an end. Following the publication of Kempe's research society began to perceive and treat child abuse as a serious social problem (Pfohl 1977; Best 1989). The concept of the "battered child syndrome" focused attention on the victim, an innocent child, and helped gain public attention to child abuse and garner sympathy for the victims. Kempe's work and the research and writings of other "claimsmakers" resulted in the rediscovery of child abuse as crucial problem in American society.

Subsequent studies have revealed that it was and is far more widespread than most people imagined (Crewdson 1988, 224). Since the 1970s surveys, studies, and coverage of abuse cases by the media have revealed child abuse to be a significant social problem. By 1976 reports of child abuse and neglect had risen to 416,000 a year. By 1992 the reported numbers had risen to 2.9 million a year (Myers 1994, 29). Overall, reports of child mistreatment had increased by an average of 6% annually since 1985 (Myers 94, 29). Since its recognition stories of child abuse have appeared regularly in the media. High profile cases such as the McMartin Preschool, the Little Rascals Pre-school, priests such as John Foster in the Catholic Church, and numerous court cases in which the dysfunctional family and abusive relationships have become part of popular culture and talk show culture. This means that in a culture that is frequently described as "child centered" numerous children are the victims of physical and sexual abuse.

Following the publication of the reports and claims made by medical researchers and pediatric radiologists about the "battered child syndrome" society began to perceive and treat child abuse as a social problem. The year Kempe and his colleagues published their article describing the "battered child syndrome" the Children's Bureau of the U.S. Department of Health, Education and Welfare sponsored a conference on child abuse. The conferees recommended adoption of laws that would require professionals to report suspected child abuse and neglect to appropriate authorities. These reporting laws wrenched the secret of abuse out of the dark and into the light of day, where it could not be ignored. As a result of these persuasive claims about the physical and sexual abuse of children protective legislation was enacted. Between 1963 and 1967, every state passed a child abuse reporting bill (Pleck, 173).

To encourage the public to report abuse, many states also established telephone hotlines and commissioned television and radio advertising to promote awareness of the problem. The Child Abuse Prevention and Treatment Act of 1974 was passed. The Act was the first national legislation to address the problem of the physical and sexual abuse of children. It created fiscal incentives for states to establish child abuse prevention programs and encouraged the enactment of child abuse reporting laws. Teachers, school administrators, and physicians, became so called "mandated reporters," required by law in all fifty states to report any suspicion of child abuse because they are in a position to detect it. They may do so anonymously and may not be held civilly liable for the consequences of their reports. These reforms have led to an increased participation of children in the legal system as victims, perpetrators, and witnesses.

In their own homes, in day care centers, with parents, sitters, or strangers, children are, as never before likely to be witnesses to a crime or be the victim of a crime. The increase in custody and adoption disputes has also increased the appearances of children in courtroom. Children may also appear in court as bystander witnesses to assaults as well as witnesses in their litigation against adults. The increase in reported abuse crimes and recent legislative changes has created a concomitant rise in the numbers of cases involving children being called as witnesses in the courts. These cases confront the legal system with situations that it was not designed for.

What David Finkelhor has called "the child protection movement" contends that the adversary system is overwhelmingly weighted against the child. They hold that confrontation with the legal system is a second and separate trauma, a process of revictimization. The argument is often made (Dezwirek-Sas, 183) that the negative emotional effects evident in child witnesses parallel those which have been documented on adult female rape victims when they testify and are revictimized in court. As in a rape trial the child's credibility is disbelieved and attacked, opening the child to further emotional trauma (Goodman, 1984). Critics of the legal system such Dzeich and Schudson argue that it does not provide justice for child abuse victims, and that, in many cases involvement in proceedings add insult to injury by reabusing children and demoralizing their families. Dziech and Schudson (4) claim that "American courts have generally regarded child victims with indifference and disbelief. That so pervasive are these attitudes that the legal system has often precluded the entry of children as witnesses in the courts and has thus increased their victimization by adults."

Although the legal system has been increasingly compelled to acknowledge the presence of children, the courts are the product of a process that until recently has been ill-equipped to deal with child witnesses and child victims. The purpose of the legal system is to settle disputes and redress wrongs. The actors in the American court system have been those with a legal status (adults not children), those who had legal interests recognized by society, and those who are able to express their interests in courts. The legal system was invented by adults with adult witnesses and suspects in mind. Historical examination of the American legal system reveals that children had almost no role in the courts in the past as defendants, plaintiffs, or witnesses. In settling disputes and redressing wrongs, children had almost nothing to do with the courts. Even when their existence was acknowledged (Dziech and Schudson, 23) in court records, it was for reasons related to the status or welfare of adults. The practical reality of social and legal life of children in the past Dziech and Schudson note (23) was "the habitual indifference to children."

A strong social base (the women's movement, experts, parents) and an evocative symbolic structure have helped to make child protection a significant social issue (Finkelhor 1994, 4). Increased awareness and responsiveness to child abuse, child sexual abuse, domestic violence, spousal battering, and divorce have led to the frequent appearance of children in the courtroom. Child abuse is often difficult to prove in court. Maltreatment occurs in secret, and the child is usually the only eyewitness. Children's testimony is often the cornerstone of child sexual abuse litigation.

The plight of children in the courtroom has recently generated considerable attention in the United States. Child protection advocates have criticized the treatment of children witness in the traditional legal system on a number of grounds. These include lack of legal knowledge, long delays before the trial, unsuitable court facilities, and the demands of an adversarial trial. Defense strategies often are seen as antithetical to a genuine search for truth. The inordinate complexity of evaluating charges and successfully prosecuting cases when witnesses are very young and when physical evidence is limited or nonexistent make it necessary to employ contemporary knowledge of child development in courtrooms so that children have an opportunity to be heard. They point to the difficulty of providing fair and full evidence to juries in abuse cases in which the only sources of evidence are either the testimony of the victim or the corroborating testimonies of others not present at the assault. They feel that there is an urgent need for courts to accommodate new techniques and new sources of evidence in the criminal justice system. The following section exams some of the issues that have arisen with the increased number of children involved in court proceedings.

Issues in Court Proceedings

In many cases, due to the lack of physical evidence or corroborating witnesses, the prosecutor's case rests in large part on the testimony of the child victim. In recent years the rules of criminal evidence in the United States (and other Western countries) have been attacked by the child protection movement for making it needlessly hard for children to be heard as witnesses, or if they are heard to be believed (Dzeich and Schudson 1989; Myer 1987). The demands of the legal system, child protection advocates hold, do not meet the needs of children. The following matters, in particular, have been the subject of repeated comment, primarily by child advocates in the child protection movement who charge that the proceedings of the legal system has revictimized victims of child abuse.

Issue: Court Milieu

Many critics have argued that most courtrooms are by their very nature unsuitable for conducting examinations of younger children and victims (Flin et al, 1992). Courtrooms were designed for the large numbers of adults who become participants and spectators in trials. Their furniture, lighting, acoustics, and uniformed personnel assure a serious, and in some ways an intimidating atmosphere. The assumption is that in such an environment, witnesses and jurors will be more likely to take their responsibilities seriously. For children however, a courtroom can terrify and silence (Dziech and Schudson, 170).

Judges usually adjust the time of the trial to accommodate the complicated schedules of lawyers. Trial schedules rarely accommodate the naptime and mealtime routines and the special rhythms of children. The passage of time can have a more adverse effect on child witnesses. With the passage of time, many witnesses may lose interest, face intimidation, or forget (Dezwirek-Sas, 1992). When children are witnesses, delays can have an even greater impact on the outcome of a trial, for in addition to the typical disadvantages of delays, there is the more compelling consideration of the amount of stress a young witness can endure.

Courtrooms are designed for grownups who can sit for long periods and engage in verbal combat without betraying fatigue or hesitation. This simply is not possible with children. They fidget after relatively short periods. They grow hungry and tired and disoriented long before adults. Thus, children are at an enormous disadvantage if their testimony is judged by individuals employing unexamined assumptions about the physical demeanor of child witnesses (Dziech and Schudson, 66).

Additionally some critics have charged that attorneys who represent the Department of Social Services are often newly minted out of law school and that the turnover rate is high, that such cases are often investigated by beginners and litigated by beginners. Several studies have found representation to be of poor quality. In New York Hechler (1985) found that 45 per cent of representation was "seriously inadequate or marginally adequate" and just 4 percent was effective.

Issue: Competency and the Competency Hearing

One of the principal concerns about children as witnesses is that they are disadvantaged compared with adults in terms of their relative ability to understand court proceedings, to cope with the emotional demands of a trial and to give competent evidence. Until recently children were judged not competent to testify in court (Dziech and Schudson, 134). In earlier times judges often ruled that children could not testify as witnesses (Myers, 1992). Children were said to be testimonially incompetent. Excluding child witness precluded an essential source of testimony. The rule prohibited prosecution in many cases

The competency hearing is the most obvious example of a special barrier the legal system has historically imposed on child witnesses too young to manage abstractions. Underlying the competency test is the theory that witnesses under a certain age must be able to prove their ability to discriminate truth from falsehood. The result has been that young children have been required to explain to judges the meaning of complex ideas and practices such as truth and oaths, right and wrong, and reality and unreality. (Dziech and Schudson, 69).

On principle, most evidence in criminal proceedings in the United States had to be under oath, and no one was permitted to take an oath unless they understood what was meant by one (Dziech and Schudson, 133). Whereas an adult was presumed to have this level of understanding a child under the age of 14 was not, and had to be questioned on the subject by the judge before being permitted to give evidence.

Since many cases of child abuse—especially sexual abuse have no witnesses other than the child and the abuser and leave no clear physical evidence, the child's memories are often the only evidence available to prosecutors. Research at the beginning of this century produced dramatic demonstrations of children suggestibility in laboratory and courtroom (Dent, 2). This work helped to contribute to the concept of the child as a dangerously suggestible witness, who, by, implication, would be less reliable than an adult witness.

These early studies did not produce comparable data from adult subjects and it was until the work of Loftus and colleagues (Loftus, 1975) that data emerged to show just how unreliable and suggestible that adults could be. In recent years there has been a gradual reassessment of children's cognitive capacities with the result that researchers are generally more optimistic about the quality of memory of children as young as three or four years and their potential as witnesses (Davies and Westcott, 212). One important conclusion to be drawn from these studies is that children as young as six years can be as reliable as adults when answering both object and suggestive question (Dent, 3).

Child protection advocates hold that one set of witnesses should not be excluded from the truth seeking process, that all doubts about a child's testimony should be resolved in favor of permitting the child to take the witness stand. They advocate the modernization of competency rules to make it easier for children to give testimony in court. Since the passage of the Victims of Child Abuse Act in 1990 children have been presumed to be competent witnesses under federal law. Today, children are usually allowed to testify, and children as young as 3 years old take the witness stand. Additional to the disadvantage occasioned by rules of evidence are the negative beliefs and attitudes of some professionals and jurors toward the ability of the child witness (Dziech and Schudson, 133). Competency rules have been reformed making it easier for children to take part in the competency hearing and subsequent trials.

Issue: The Adversarial Examination

Where the child passes the competency examination, the next problem has always been that on principle he or she has to give evidence under the same conditions as an adult—testifying live, on the day of the trial, in open court, in the presence of the defendant, and then subjecting himself or herself to an adversarial cross-examination. These conditions are stressful for many adults. They prevent many children from giving evidence at all. John Myers (172) contends that "It is undoubtedly true that many children are traumatized by multiple interviews, testifying in open, court, cross-examination, and face-to-face confrontation with their abuser." There are several potential problems with the adversarial process that child advocates have drawn attention to.

Child victims are often pressured by perpetrators to remain silent, and there are sometimes threats of harm to the child or the child's parents (Flin et al, 1992). Children are often inhibited from reporting the abuse initially and often have difficulty repeating what happened over and over through the investigation, preparation for prosecution, preliminary hearings, and the trial. If pressure is applied by family members and others who may sympathize with the abuser, the child may well recant. Even if the child is supported, there are likely to be some inconsistencies if the child is required to repeat a story that may have its beginnings several years earlier. The limitations of children's verbal skills may jeopardize their credibility as witnesses.

Difficulties could emerge as a result of questions being put to the child by the lawyer which were age-inappropriate in terms of either vocabulary or grammar. The lawyer needs to be able to understand the language of children and to be able to communicate with children, not in the esoteric language of the law, but in language appropriate to the particular state of the child's development. This is especially important in sexual abuse cases, where the child's terminology for body parts can be very different from that of an adult. Dezwirek-Sas (187) quotes a 10 year old girl who defined a subpoena as "a male private part" and others have found that pre-school children pointed to their ears and arms when asked to indicate their private parts.

In the legal system terminology is paramount. It is the business of lawyers to master artifice to manipulate or to establish clarity. A successful witness must be able to listen carefully and maintain attention for significant periods of time. He or she must have the cognitive and verbal skills to decipher attorneys' questions, reconstruct events, recall previous statements from various stages of legal process, and relate a story to a judge and jury. Ideally, he or she will not be intimated by a new environment, by the presence of the offender, or by the demeanor and legal tactics of hostile attorneys.

With little social experience of any kind and limited verbal skills and cognitive development, many sexual abuse victims find it impossible to produce a "conventional story." In sexual abuse cases, the child has to succeed at least in telling the substance of the story to the jury, or there is no case. Adult perpetrators usually have the cognitive ability, experience, and motivation to construct versions of past events (Dent, 1992). Children are not so adept. Thus when judges and juries evaluate their stories on their abilities to provide coherent descriptions of events surrounding assaults, children suffer enormous disadvantages. In order to be believed, witnesses must not only possess certain cognitive skills but also the linguistic abilities to understand attorneys and communicate effectively. Because so few judges or jurors understand the differences in the linguistic capacities of children and adults, attorneys are seldom required to accommodate question of children to their unique capacities.

Young children find it difficult to understand to and explain time, distance and speed (Dent, 1992). When asked if two weeks elapsed between one event and another most young children witnesses find it impossible to reply to adult's satisfaction (Dzeich and Schudson, 69). Children can rarely remember in what month an event occurred and often have difficulty recounting how long an event lasted (Hechler, 68) Since so much depends upon witnesses' being able to place events in time, defense lawyers can easily destroy children's credibility by exposing inaccuracies in their attempts to place events in proper sequence.

The typical investigative procedures involve repeated interviews by authorities and mental health professionals. This experience may create confusion of fact and fantasy, elicit ever greater incursion into the realm of fantasy, and train the child to please adults by giving them what they want.

Issue: Rules Against Hearsay

Hearsay testimony is often not allowed as evidence. Hearsay is an out-of-court statement that is not made under oath, is not subject to cross-examination, and is offered for its truth. A prominent feature of the law of criminal evidence is the rule against hearsay. This provides that a fact may not be established by A, who did not see or hear it, to tell the court that he heard B, who did describe it. Either B must be called to describe it to the court or the incident must be proved by other means. The importance of hearsay in child sexual abuse cases is that if a parent, teacher, therapist, or doctor is permitted to repeat what a child said concerning an allegation, the child may be spared the trauma of a having to repeat the story in a court room of strangers.

The hearsay rule when taken in conjunction with the competency requirement, can cause great difficulties in child abuse cases. The competency requirement prevents the court from hearing an account of the incident from the mouth of the child itself, and the hearsay rule stops the court hearing an account second hand from adults. Just as the search for truth should assure children the chance to testify, the child advocacy movement claims it should also assure that in some cases their voices be heard through hearsay rather than in person. These issues discussed above have led to legislative, technological and judicial reforms.

Legislative, Judicial, and Technological Reforms

By most sociological standards the mobilization around child abuse and the plight of children witnesses were very successful social problem mobilizations. They reached a wide audience and galvanized a great deal of professional public policy activity. A great deal of government and professional activity has been generated. Social institutions like the courts have been visibly affected. In the past few years some significant changes have been made, and it is no longer true that children must give evidence under exactly the same conditions as adults. There have been significant, legislative, judicial, and technological reforms.

Media attention to the issue of the revictimization and traumatization of abused children gave rise to increased public concern which was translated into legislative action. Law-makers and practitioners in a number of different western countries are attempting to decide upon and implement more effective policies for child victims. These changes can be grouped into two categories. The first includes those items which can be put into practice now with little or no fundamental legal or procedural reform required. Such innovations include modifications in courtroom formalities, increased education and broader based training of professionals and those who work with the children, changing the way children are interviewed, and the preparation of children for testimony.

The second category involves changes in the procedures which require a much more essential change in traditional practice. In the Victims of Child Abuse Act of 1990, the federal government endorsed a number of rights and protections for child victims and witnesses (Whitcomb, 152), including:

  -Alternative to live in-court testimony, whether by two-way closed circuit television at trial or by videotaped depositions
  -Presumption of children's competency as witnesses
  -Privacy protection from public identification
  -Closing the courtroom during the children's testimony
  -Victim impact statements from children
  -Appointment of guardians ad litem to protect the best interests of child victims
  -Appointment of a child's attendant to provide emotional support for children during judicial proceedings
  -Extension of the statute of limitations for commencing prosecution of child sexual or physical abuse allegations until the child reaches the age of 25
  -Testimonial aids, such as dolls, puppets, or drawings

There have also been a number of significant procedural reforms such as the elimination of special competency requirements for child witnesses in many states.

Another category of courtroom reform includes statutes that create special exceptions to the hearsay rules for out-of-court statement made by child sexual abuse victims. Under American jurisprudence out-of-court statements are usually not admissible in court (Myer, 1987). It is not uncommon, however, for young sexual abuse victims to make remarks either naively or while being examined by a professional that quite explicitly describe sexual activities that should be unknown to a child or particular events. Their reaction may be as matter-of-fact as that of the seven year old girl who casually said to her father, "Daddy, does milk come out of your weiner: It comes out of Uncle Bob's and it tastes yukky" (qtd in Dziech and Schudson, 143). Child advocates propose that the hearsay rules be waived under certain circumstances. Thus John E.B. Myers advocates that special exceptions to the hearsay statements of children such as "the excited utterance exception," be enacted by legislatures and courts (Myers 1994, 45). Recognizing that children are often functionally unavailable to testify, hearsay exception laws developed over the years to allow others to tell juries what children said had happened to them. At least 28 states have created a special exception precisely crafted to permit such statements by children into testimony.

Judicial Reform and Technological Reform

These statutes which provide protections for children in the legal system and provide for alternative procedures for dealing with children in the courtroom have generally been upheld by the courts. In 1995 the Supreme Court held in Wheeler v. the United States (in which the defendant appealed his conviction for murder, claiming the five-year old child of the victim should not have been allowed to testify) that:

> The boy was not by reason of his youth, as a matter of law, absolutely disqualified as a witness is clear...There is no precise age which determines the question of competency. This depends on the capacity and intelligence of the child, his appreciation of the difference between truth and falsehood, as well as of his duty to tell the former. The decision of this question rests primarily with the trial judge...To exclude (a child) from the witness stand...would sometimes result in staying the hand of justice (qtd in Dziech and Schudson, 133–134).

Although there are some exceptions the trend has been away from the old competency rule and to permit the child to take the witness stand. In 1974, the revised Federal Rules of Evidence abolished the competency rule for trials in the federal courts. In recent decisions such as Kentucky v. Stincer (1987) the Supreme Court has declared that the constitutional rights of defendants must coexist with the opportunity for children to testify.

The use of hearsay evidence that comes from children has been upheld provided they are tailored to meet certain requirements set forth in Ohio v. Roberts (448 U.S. 56 1980). In Roberts the Court held that statements made by children were allowable if "the time, content, and circumstances of the statement provide sufficient indicia of reliability" to be given to the jury. In allowing such hearsay evidence the judge is not telling the jury the hearsay is true, only that it should hear the testimony and decide for itself. Later in United States v. Inadi (1986) the Court allowed the admissibility of statements even if the witness could testify his or her self.

However, in a 1990 5-4 decision, the US Supreme Court imposed some important limitations on the admissibility of children's out of court statements (Idaho v. Wright 110 SC. 3139 (1990)). In that case, a child's statements made to a pediatrician had been admitted in a trial court after a finding that the child was incapable of communicating with the jury and was therefore unavailable to testify. In Idaho v. Wright the Supreme Court found that admission of a child's hearsay statements violated the Confrontation Clause of the Constitution.

In this case respondent Laura Wright was charged with lewd conduct with a minor, specifically her 5 ½ and 2 ½ year old daughters. She was convicted of restraining and silencing her daughters while the daughter's father abused them. At the trial, it was agreed that the younger daughter was not capable of communicating with the jury. However, the court allowed, under Idaho's residual hearsay exception, some statements that she had made to a physician who had had extensive experience in child abuse cases. The doctor testified that she had reluctantly given answers to question about her own abuse, but had spontaneously volunteered information about her older sister's abuse. Wright was convicted on both counts in the trial court, but appealed only the conviction involving the younger child.

In ruling that it was an error for the trial court to admit the child's hearsay statement, the Supreme Court found that the child's statement to the doctor lacked sufficient guarantees of trust worthiness to satisfy the reliability requirement set forth in Roberts. The Court noted that the child's statements did not fall within the traditional hearsay exception and lacked "particular guarantees of trustworthiness" because the doctor had conducted the interview without procedural safeguards such as videotaping the interview. The Court also found that the hearsay statements did not bear "adequate indicia of reliability," noting that the doctor had asked leading questions and had a preconceived idea of what the child should be disclosing.

In measuring the "indicia of reliability" the Court concluded that such circumstances "include only those that surround the making of a statement: and not other evidence that corroborates the statement. Among the criteria that had contributed to the lower court's decision to admit the child's statement, the Supreme Court accepted only two as related to the reliability of the statement; whether the child had a motive to fabricate the allegations, and whether the child's description of the alleged abuse was consistent with the cognitive abilities and sexual awareness of so young a child (Whitcomb, 157). Physical evidence of abuse, corroborating statements from another witness, and opportunity for the defendant to commit the abuse—all were rejected as not pertinent to the making of the statement itself and therefore inappropriate in weighing its reliability. The State's contention that evidence corroborating a hearsay statement may properly support a finding was rejected since that would permit admission of presumptively unreliable statements, such as those made under duress. Thus, Whitcomb, points out (157) the existence of corroborating evidence may not be considered in determining whether a child's statement possesses particularized guarantees of trustworthiness; rather prosecutors must search for indicators surrounding the making of the statement itself.

Other changes in court room procedures involve a more essential change in traditional practices. Technology has now broadened the options for protecting children as witnesses. One of the most controversial issues to emerge from recent concern over the plight of child witnesses has been the use of video technology in the court room. Videotape and closed circuit television offer children the chance to testify in court without being in the courtroom. It is argued that videotape and closed circuit television can act as an additional source of support for the child's testimony if the child must testify.

Many states have adopted laws that permit alternative techniques to alleviate the perceived stress on children when they testify (Dezwirek-Sas, 182). The goal is to improve the experiences of child victims in the court through the provision of modifications in court procedures. Perhaps the most radical of these measures are those that attempt to shield the child from direct confrontation by the accused in court: broadcasting the child's live testimony to the courtroom via closed circuit television, videotaping the child's testimony at a deposition apart from the trial itself, or erecting a screen in the courtroom.

In recent years, responding to efforts to spare children the trauma of court testimony, many states have enacted laws allowing children to be in court through videotaped depositions. Videotape replaces the child's testimony, thus removing the need for the child to appear in court. Videotaping has been used both for investigative interviews and for taking depositions. If children's live evidence is replaced with a video recording, they will not have to testify in an unfamiliar and public place about a frightening and possibly embarrassing experience, and are less likely to be intimated by their surroundings or the presence of the alleged perpetrator (Dzeich and Schudson, 1989). The practices have been supported on the grounds that they are "hearsay exceptions" and that they are "functional equivalents" of in court testimony. Another benefit which some have suggested is that it may encourage guilty pleas from defendants who have viewed the tape (Whitcomb et al, 1985).

The use of closed circuit television to separate the child physically from the accused during testimony has been pioneered in the United States. State legislatures began to introduce provision for the use of video links for children in criminal trials in 1983 (Davies and Waistcoat 212) and now some 29 states have such legislation on their statute books. Subsequently, Canada, Australia, New Zealand and the United Kingdom have all moved to permit testimony to be given in this way (Davies and Waistcoat, 212). With closed-circuit television, children can testify in comfortable settings that preserve appropriate court procedure. The practice has also grown up of allowing child witnesses to give evidence from behind a screen that blocks her/him form having to look at the defendant as they testify.

Set against the particular difficulties children often experience in testifying effectively in court, video technology and the use of one way screens seems to offer significant advantages. It could eliminate confrontation with the defendant, one of the major fears expressed by child witnesses who are called to court (Davies and Waistcoat, 212). Another perceived benefit of the system is that the child need never have sight of the accused throughout his or her testimony. By testifying from a small room with social support, anxiety about speaking out in court, with its alien, adult and often intimidating setting may be reduced. At the beginning of the nineties 31 states had enacted legislation permitting the use of closed circuit television and 36 had provided for videotaped deposition as alternatives to in-court testimony. Twenty-two states provided for both forms of alternative testimony, only seven states provided for neither (Whitcomb, 153).

The arguments for the use of video technology have not gone unchallenged. Attitudes toward the use of video technology are sharply differentiated between those who place significance on the importance of confrontation and those who give primacy to oral evidence. Several potential problems arise when the child's testimony is transmitted through a video link or is recorded. The first of these is the contention that the use of video link deprives the defendant of the right to confront the witness. This "right" of physical confrontation is strongly entrenched in American law (Davies and Waistcoat, 220). By blocking direct confrontation between victim and accused, these techniques, critics argue, pose a serious threat to the Sixth Amendment to the United States Constitution, which guarantees every defendant the right to confront his/her accusers face to face; "In all criminal prosecutions, the accused shall enjoy the right…to be confronted with the witnesses against him."

Another legal concern (Davies and Waistcoat 217) is the impact of the withdrawal of the witness from the court on the perceived guilt of the accused: is the accused too dangerous to be allowed near the child? A judge will often instruct a jury that they should draw no pejorative implication from the child's use of closed circuit television in these circumstances. However, it is unclear whether this is sufficient to eliminate prejudice in the eyes of the jury (Myers, 1987). State courts have upheld the use of closed circuit television. In 1987 the Pennsylvania Superior Court affirmed a sexual assault conviction when a five-year old child testified by closed circuit after she "froze emotionally and was unable to testify in the presence of her father." The court explained that the "right to confront does not confer upon the accused the right to intimidate" (qtd. in Dziech and Schudson, 155). As cases resulting from these laws have made their way to the Supreme Court the Court has begun to provide some guidance on this issue.

The first case to reach the US Supreme Court on the issue of alternative to in-court testimony involved a screen with "one-way" glass which had been erected in the courtroom between the child witnesses and the defense table during the child's testimony. In a case involving the sexual abuse of two thirteen-year old girls the Iowa trial judge allowed the two girls to testify from behind a one-way screen. The defendant could see the girls, and his lawyer could cross-examine them, but the girls could not see the defendant sitting in the courtroom.

Reversing the guilty conviction, the Court in Coy v. Iowa (1988) reiterated that the Sixth Amendment right of confrontation entails at least a strong preference that confrontation between a witness and defendant be "face-to-face." In Coy (487 U.S. 1012 (1988)) the Court acknowledged that the right of confrontation is not absolute, and could give way to "other important interests." In Coy the Court concluded that Iowa's statute, which created a generalized presumption of trauma to child witnesses, was insufficient to justify an exception to the Confrontation Clause (Whitcomb, 153). Instead the Court set a standard that would require "individualized findings that these particular witnesses needed special protection". The Iowa judge allowed use of this special device without first reviewing whether, in fact, the two girls required the assistance of this special technique. It would be necessary the Court insinuated to show that the child would suffer severe emotional damage by testifying in open court.

In Maryland v. Craig (1990) the Court ruled on an appeal of a Maryland Court of Appeals decision in which applying the "high threshold" suggested in Coy found that children must first be questioned in the presence of the defendant (to assess whether they would be traumatized), and secondarily by way of two-way closed circuit television, before the more restrictive one-way procedure could be used (Craig v. State, 316 Md. Ct. App. 1989). The Supreme Court disagreed with this interpretation. In Maryland v. Craig, (110. S.Ct 3157 (1990) the Court found that the Maryland statute, which requires a determination that the child will suffer serious emotional distress such that the child cannot reasonably communicate, clearly suffices to meet constitutional standards.

In Maryland v. Craig the court ruled that the Confrontation Clause did not require confrontation if other due process traditions were followed including testimony under oath and full cross examination. The Confrontation Clause therefore did not guarantee criminal defendants an absolute right to a face to face meeting with the witnesses against them at trial. The trial court must determine on a case specific basis whether a particular child would be traumatized by testifying in the presence of a defendant.

Although the Court declined to articulate a minimum standard for the finding of emotional trauma, it did offer some clarification. Before an alternative to direct confrontation can be permitted, the Court held, there must be a showing that the child will be traumatized, not by the courtroom generally, but by the defendant's presence, and further, the child's emotional distress will be "more than *de minimus*."

In its discussion, the Court delineated four elements of confrontation: physical presence of the witness, testifying under oath, cross-examination, and observation of the witness's demeanor by the trier of fact. According to the Court, closed circuit television incorporates all these elements thereby serving as the "functional equivalent" of live, in court testimony (Whitcomb, 154). In Craig the Court appears to have opened the door for greater use of alternative videotechnology to testimony in open court for child witnesses. So far, the actual use of the equipment has been less frequent that was originally anticipated by advocates (Davies and Waistcoat, 214). However, it remains to be seen how the Appeal courts will operationalize this requirement, along with the showing that the child's stress will be more than "*de minimus*."[3]

At the beginning of 1989 15 states had enacted legislation making videotaped statements or interviews with child witnesses admissible at trial under certain circumstances. Salient features of these laws include questioning of the child by a non-attorney; availability of the interviewer for direct and cross-examination at trial; and availability of the child to testify at trial.

These statutes clearly do not contemplate videotape as an alternative to in court testimony, since the child must be available for trial. Rather, protecting the child from the presumed trauma of trial testimony appears to be an implicit agenda. In practice the defense can call the child for cross examination. However, many defense attorneys choose not to call the child for fear of angering a jury that may be sympathetic to the child's plight. Defense lawyers often claim that it would not be in their interests to be seen putting a child under stress in the witness-box, since it might well lose them the sympathy of the court (Flin, 177) As a result, the videotape of a child's statement given to a law enforcement officer, social worker, or mental health professional may stand as the only evidence provided by the child.

Conclusion: Legal, Political, and
Social Consequences of Children as Witnesses

Awareness of the potential evidential contribution of children has been growing apace (Dent and Flin, 1992). Despite an historical neglect of and bias against the child witness (Dziech and Schudson 1989; Goodman 1984) in the last decade there has been increasing participation of children in the legal system. This participation combined with public awareness and concern has led to many fundamental changes in the legal and political status of the child witness and the social status of children.

The introduction of legal, judicial, and technological reforms arose from a genuine concern to ease the ordeal of the child witness giving evidence in court. An increasing body of informed research on children as witnesses has been rapidly accumulating. Legal reforms and video-technology have opened up new prospects as well as new problems for those who deal with child witnesses. There is an increasing awareness and consideration of the rights of victims to be spared revictimization. And searching questions are being asked and contemporaneous discussions are raising the rights of the victim as well as the rights of the defendants.

However as public concern about child abuse has heightened, denial of the problem and resistance to legal reforms have increased in some quarters. There is a growing "backlash" against child protection (Myers 1994, 17). Starting in the late 1980's and extending to the present there have been strong signs of a "backlash" (Heckler 1988; Myers 1994) to many of the reforms that grew out of the successes of the child protection movement. David Hechler describes the emergence of a "backlash" against the recognition of child abuse as a serious problem:

> One thing is clear; there is a war. There are those who feel that the country is suffering from an epidemic of child sexual abuse and those who feel that there is an epidemic all right, but not of sex abuse—"sex accuse," as some have disparagingly called it. The pendulum has swung too far, they say, and what we see now is a blizzard of false accusations. (3)

The "backlash" can be described as a response to the child protection movement— in particular to the growth in the number of reports of abuse and state interventions in recent years. The "backlash" includes wide ranging attacks on the field of child protection advocacy and many of the reforms discussed in the previous section of this paper. This position finds what it calls "the child abuse industry" (Wimberly 1994, 47) to be self-serving—over dramatizing the problem, child protection workers to be zealots trampling the rights of innocent citizens—often "brainwashing" children, and courts engaged in hysterical witch hunts against innocent victims.

While child protection advocates like Dziech, Schudson, and Myers see a court system that unnecessarily traumatizes and discounts child witnesses in protecting the accused, the "backlash" holds a diametrically opposed view. They describe nightmares of false accusation, relaxed standards of evidence, and the abrogation of fundamental legal rights (Wexler 1990). This distrust of the systems presumption of the innocence of the child and the lack of protection of the defendant's rights is reflected in Douglas Besharov's (qtd. in Wakefield and Underwager, x) statement that society believes alleged child abusers to have "a lesser right to the presumption of innocence." Critics such as Hollida Wakefield and Ralph Underwager (1988) see a corrupt and inept bureaucracy too eager to prosecute the innocent.

A prime example of this viewpoint is the organization known as Victims of Child Abuse Laws, VOCAL. VOCAL was founded in 1984 by parents who claimed to have been wrongfully accused of child abuse (Wimberly 1994, 49). VOCAL members argue that the current child protection system is out of control, and that many innocent people are caught up in a web of unfounded and false accusations. The court system, VOCAL believes, treats those accused of child abuse as if they were guilty. "Once accused of child abuse," Wimberly contends (50) "an individual is treated as though he or she is guilty. There is no more presumption of innocence. The burden of proof seems to be on the parents rather than on state where it belongs."

From VOCAL and other independent sources a new literature has emerged which has attempted to draw public attention to problems that have resulted from recent reforms. These various claimsmakers have sought to use persuasive communication to persuade and convince others that there are significant problems in the reforms that have been adopted to protect children as witness. They have attempted to expose what they see as abuses and problems with the increased access that children have to the legal system. Several themes emerge from VOCAL, media coverage of child abuse stories, and books on child abuse cases.

One common theme in the "backlash" literature is that the child protection system is dangerously out of control. As Richard Wexler (1990) writes in *Wounded Innocents: The Real Victims of the War Against Child Abuse*:

> We have turned almost everyone who deals with children in the course of his or her work into an informer, required to report any suspicion of any form of child maltreatment, and we have encouraged the general public to do the same. We have allowed such reports to be made anonymously, making the system a potent tool for harassment (175).

Wexler's book is only one of many describing the nightmare of false accusations and a system that is on an irresponsible rampage. In *The Abuse of Innocence* Paul Eberle and Shirley Eberle (408) hold that "The child abuse industry has spun out of control and become a voracious monster, hungry for human sacrifice, devouring everything in its path." Recent documentaries on the Little Rascals Day Care Center, Repressed Memory Syndrome on Public Television and books such as Lawrence Wright's *Remembering Satan* and Michael Yapko's *Suggestions of Abuse* portray the current child protection system on an irresponsible rampage.

A second theme is to portray allegations of abuse as a witch hunt. Many critics have drawn the analogy between contemporary child protection and the Salem witchcraft trials. Indeed one critic wrote a book title *Sex Abuse Hysteria: Salem*

Witch Trials Revisited (Gardner 1991). Such critics draw several parallels between Salem and 20th century child protection. In Salem innocent people were convicted as witches and burned at the stake. Today, critics assert that innocent people are branded as child abusers and punished. Today, children's testimony is the most important evidence in many sexual abuse cases. In Salem children's testimony was used to convict innocent people of witchcraft. Today children's testimony is seen to lead to the conviction of innocent people of child abuse.

Another claim is that there is reason to fear that improper interviewing leads some children into false accusations (Ceci and Bruck, 1993). In experiments with children Ceci and others find children reporting events, such as body parts being touched, when in fact no such events occurred. In late 1993 the highly publicized conviction of day care teacher Kelly Michaels was reversed in part because of the way the preschool-age children were interviewed (State v. Michaels, 1993).

An evocative symbolic structure, an effective use of the image of the child as innocent victim and unreliable victimizer helps to explain why both children protection and the backlash have been so successful as social problem mobilizations. Social problem movements, even successful ones face resistance. The "backlash" is fairly oppositional and reactive; it has little in its agenda beside complaints about professional practices and legal practices. It is narrowly focused, largely attacking means rather than ends. Will this movement become powerful and influential? Although its claimsmakers have made some effective arguments it has not as yet had any significant policy impact. And the public is more concerned about abusers who go free than about people who are unfairly prosecuted.

NOTES

1.   In *Making an Issue of Child Abuse*, Barbara J. Nelson pointed out that during the decade prior to the Kempe article, all the relevant professions (medicine, law, education, and the social sciences) produced only 9 articles on child abuse. In the decade following the Kempe article 260 articles appeared, and during the 1980's there have been thousands of publications and media presentations on the issue. Nelson observed (51) that public concern was finally aroused because the media "created and responded to the urgency over child abuse."

2.   In order for doctors to report such incidents they must entertain the possibility that such a condition exists. As Pfohl has noted many doctors have not been trained to diagnose suspected abuse. Moreover, children are only nominally the pediatrician's clients. The real clients are the parents who pay the bills. Reporting child sexual abuse can be bad for business. Significantly a number of studies have found that doctors in private practice report sexual abuse less often than doctors in public clinics or hospital emergency rooms (Hechler, 27).

3.   The medical discovery of child abuse was initiated by pediatric radiologists studying the X-rays of children who had suffered fractures, or blows to the skull. Pediatric radiologists were not deterred by parental explanations, did not have the parents as clients, were
not bound by doctor patient confidentiality, were deterred by fear of libel suits, or fearful of
participation in the criminal justice system. Thus, radiological evidence cold cast doubt on
the claim of a parent or guardian that a child had not been previously injured.

CHAPTER FOUR
The Media's Focus on the Child

The transformed significance of the child in society is evident not only in the issues previously examined; studies of the historical status of childhood, the symbolic use childhood in social theory, and the changing courtroom status of the child, but in two recent phenomena as well; the shining of the media spotlight on particular children and the media attention and concern given to children's social issues. In this chapter we'll briefly examine the phenomena of children becoming widely covered stories in the media, and some of the ways that media has been instrumental in transforming the status of children.

The Child as an Object of Media Attention

As Chapter I notes, social concern for children is not new. Historians such as Aries, de Mause and Postman agree that modernization has increased societies concern for children's well being. Edward Shorter (1977) and Viviana Zelizer (1985) have noted how the twentieth century saw important changes in American attitudes toward children. Shorter noted "a surge of sentiment" regarding children, children became lovable, vulnerable innocents cherished for their own sakes. In her study of the changing social value of children in American society Zelizer described the "sentimentalization" of children in American society during the nineteenth and twentieth centuries. In her study Zelizer showed how the sentimentalization of child was expressed in the concern over childhood deaths in the early twentieth century leading to campaigns to promote safety and laws to reduce street accidents.

Although concern for children is not new, there has been an increase in the social awareness and concern for children's well being in the late twentieth century.
Children have become objects of media attention. Although stories involving children have been important stories in the past, such as the Dionne quintuplets and the
Lindberg baby kidnapping, in the late twentieth century widely covered stories involving children and the problems of children have become frequent and common-
place. These stories made newspaper headlines, magazine covers, the nightly news,
infotainment shows, and were often turned into made for television movies.

Images of children have played a role in child saving, social reform, and social
issues involving children, and different children have become important images in
the media and in the mind of the public. Today the media has become saturated, and
the public has become infatuated with the stories of particular children such as "Baby M," "Baby Jessica," "Baby Richard," "Baby Miranda," Elian Gonzales, Adam
Walsh, Polly Klass, and the births of multiple babies.

A number of issues involving reproduction have put children in the media spotlight. In 1978 "Louise Brown" the first successful in vitro fertilization became an
object of intense media focus. The development of surrogacy as a practice through
which infertile couples could become parents led to several highly publicized instances in which the surrogate mother decided to keep the baby. In 1987, Mary
Beth Whitehead delivered "Baby M," who she bore after being impregnated
through artificial insemination by William Stern. Despite a surrogacy contract
Whitehead refused to give up the child after birth and fled New Jersey. As Barbara
Katz Rothman noted (1990, 23) "the cry of Mary Beth Whitehead captured the attention of America and the world." The media and the court focused attention on
whether or not Mary Beth Whitehead was a suitable mother for "Baby M." The
case of "Baby M" and the image of "Baby M" Rothman observed (1990, 24) "crys-
tallized the issue of surrogacy for society and surrogacy." In the widely covered
court battle that followed Mary Beth Whitehead lost custody but was later granted
visitation rights.

A number of recent cases involving the conflict of the biological father with
adoptive parents over custody of children has led to several widely covered events
by the media. For years, fathers of out-of-wedlock children were rarely involved in
adoptions. In 1993, however, in a highly publicized case, a child given up for adoption by her biological mother was returned to her mother and her biological father
when the Iowa courts ruled favorably on a custody suit brought by the father. Three
years earlier, "Baby Jessica's" mother had agreed to let a couple in Michigan adopt
her, but when the mother told her ex-boyfriend, the child's biological father, about
the adoption, he decided to go to court to seek custody of "Baby Jessica" and won
on the grounds that under Iowa law, a father must consent to an adoption. The media images showed "Baby Jessica" "wailing inconsolably as a van sped her from the

only home she'd ever known" (*Newsweek*, March 21, 60). Her face filled magazine covers, her story became a movie of the week. A year later "Baby Jessica" now 3 year old Anna Schmidt appeared on the cover of *Newsweek* (March 21, 1994) with the caption "She's Not Baby Jessica Anymore." The following story described a family visit one year after her removal from the family that wished to adopt her.

In a somewhat similar case in 1994, the Illinois Supreme Court ruled that a three-year-old boy known as "Baby Richard" be returned to his biological parents. In this case, the biological father had been told by his former fiancée that the baby had died when the father was on a trip to his native country. When he learned that the baby was alive and had been placed for adoption, however, the father began legal action to stop the proceeding and married the baby's biological mother. In 1995 the biological parents won custody of their son. The story was widely covered by the media. Barbara Walters interviewed the adoptive parents on ABC's 20/20.

A number of other stories involving young children were also covered by newspapers, magazines, and television in the mid 1990's. In 1994 the saga of Kimberly Mays continued in the public spotlight. Kimberly Mays whose DNA tests showed had been switched in hospital nursery with a seriously ill baby 15 years earlier won a landmark legal battle when she went to court in 1993 and successfully had the court name Robert Mays who had raised her from birth, declared her "legal" and "natural" father. In 1994 she changed her mind and went to live with her biological parents. In the early nineties attention was focused on a Michigan Court which gave "Baby Miranda" to her biological father because her biological mother was attending college. In December of 1997 Bobbi McCaughey gave birth to septuplets in Des Moines Iowa drawing the media spotlight to "The Amazing McCaughey Septuplets" *(Newsweek*, December 1, 1997 cover).

"About once a day," *Newsweek* (April 10, 2000) observed, "the 6 year old boy is trotted out before the cameramen who sit outside his house all day in chairs." Elian Gonzales, a 6 year old Cuban boy who survived his mother's failed attempt to flee to the United States by boat occupied center stage in a lengthy dispute between his biological father and the Immigration and Naturalization Service and his Miami relatives. For several months pictures of the photogenic Elian at play, denouncing Cuba, being taken at gun point by Immigration and Naturalization Service agents from his Miami relatives, and returning to Cuba dominated television coverage, magazine covers, and newspaper headlines.

The image of the menaced child has also shaped public reactions to wide range of social issues. Pro life opponents of abortion have used the sonographic image of children, the hands of children, and feet of children (as well as pictures of fetuses) to attack abortion in terms of murdered children. (Neustadter, 1990). In Pro Life advocacy materials emphasis on the fetus as an "unborn child" constitutes a paradigmatic image. Photographic evidence of fetal development in their presentations often supersedes discursive argument. Mothers Against Drunk Driving (MADD) has attacked drunk drivers using commercials which depict child-victims.

In the 1990's stories and images of "crack babies" fueled attempts to regulate and punish the behavior of pregnant women (Neustadter, 1994) There were nightly news reports of inner-city intensive care units overflowing with "crack babies" where one in four children were said to be born physically and mentally stunted by fetal alcohol syndrome (Neustadter 1994, 109). There were also front-page stories reporting studies that suggested staggering rates of drug use during pregnancy. The *New York Times* reported that in 11 percent of pregnancies women used drugs during pregnancy affecting 375,000 newborns a year (Pollitt 1990, 29). These widely publicized claims were likely the basis of public fears about crack addicted babies and attempts to prosecute and convict mothers of "crack babies" and infants who were exposed to illegal drugs.

The media has also focused on some social problems of children. This has been particularly true in the case of missing children. The issue of missing children raised by social constructionists has been picked up by the media. The social constructionist study of social problems focuses on the emergence and genesis of social problems (Best 1989; Holsten and Miller 1993; Spector and Kituse 1977). Instead of trying to study the social conditions that lead to the identification of a social problem, constructionists examine the concerns that led to the identification and definition of social problems. The social constructionist tradition directs attention away from the features of a particular condition, and toward the rhetoric of "claims making." Constructionists examine how particular conditions and behaviors are brought to people's notice and become recognized as social problems (Best 1990, 11). In this view it is the process of claims making that turns conditions or circumstance, which previously may have gone unnoticed, into the focus of concern—social problems. Best has argued in books titled *Threatened Children* (1990) and *Troubling Children* (1992) that the social constructionist approach has had a major effect on the definition of social problems of children.

Significantly much constructionist analysis of social problems has been motivated by concerns about children (Best 1990; 1994). Constructionists have written about the social construction of delinquency (Platt 1969), hyperkinesis (Conrad 1975), and child abuse (Phofl 1977). Since the "discovery of child abuse" and "the battered child syndrome" American society has experienced waves of concern about various threats to children such as kidnapping, murder, abuse, neglect, and incest (Best 1994) which have then been given prominent attention by the media.

Best applies the constructionist view of social problem genesis to instances where adult groups seek to protect children, in his analysis of the concern over child abduction by strangers in the 1980's (Best, 1990). Best (23) describes several notorious cases of children being abducted and killed by strangers in the late 1970's such as Adam Walsh and Etan Patz and the victims of John Wayne Gacy and the Atlanta Child murders. Best contends the missing-children problem shows how rhetoric plays a central role in claims making about social problems. Claims-makers, Best contends, called attention to the missing-children problem by citing atrocity stories and statistics (Best 1990, 46) that placed the total number of missing children at 1.8 million per year. (Best suggests that these claims are inflated.) As a result, he argues, the cases and the statistics were given prominent attention by the media and led to child saving campaigns which led to the taking of identification pictures of children, to pictures of missing children in public service announcements, billboards, and on milk cartons. Images of missing children, often displayed by the media, television and news magazines in particular, Best holds, became a successful resource in dramatizing the problem of missing children. The media not only has focused on particular children and particular types of children, but it can be argued, has a transformative effect on children and childhood.

Marketing to Children
Children as Consumers: The commercialization of childhood

The media is not only an instrument for shining the spotlight on children and the issues of children, but in transforming children into consumers through dominating their space. When all media is combined (Schor, 33) television, radio, computers and video games, the average American child is estimated to spend about five hours and twenty-nine minutes a day with the media for a total of more than thirty eight hours a week. As several critics of the media (Schor 2004; Linn 2005) have suggested, the media, particularly television, is the instrument for marketers and corporations laying claim to children as a consumer group. Children have become the conduits from the consumer marketplace into the household. Advertisers have direct access to children because they often watch television without adult supervision. Two thirds of children between the ages of eight and eighteen have a television in their bedrooms. Thirty two percent of two to seven year olds have a television in their bedroom as do twenty six percent of children under two (Linn, 5) Marketers have also used other parent free environments, most notably school and the Internet where they can convey messages directly to children.

What was once a relatively small market dominated largely by toy companies has escalated into a large marketing enterprise (Schor, 1) with an estimated marketing budget of between 15-17 billion dollars a year, a stunning increase from the paltry $100 million spent on television advertising in 1983. The marketing seems to be worth it. According to Juliet Schor, children influence more than $600 billion in spending a year. As a result companies have created scores of surveys, polls, "cool hunters," and ethnographic studies to find the behaviors and influences on children and their consumption patterns. A significant portion of the research being conducted on the lives of children is being done by researchers funded by the corporate world. Susan Linn (2005, 26) quotes Paul Kurnit, the president of an ad agency marketing to children as saying, "We've probably done more recent original research on kids, life stages, and recognition of brands than anybody."

Heavy television advertising is targeted to children. In what Linn (2005, 1) calls "the marketing maelstrom" kids watch an estimated 40,000 commercials a year. According to the American Medical Association (Bagdikian, xxxvi) children between the ages of two and seventeen watch an average of 15,000 to 18,000 hours of television a year, more than the 12,000 hours a year spent per year in school. Research from the American Psychological Association shows that children under the age of eight are unable to critically comprehend televised advertising messages and are prone to accept advertiser messages as truthful, accurate and unbiased. Preschool children (Linn, 2) are unable to differentiate between commercials and regular programming on television. "Until the age of about eight," such children Linn contends, "can't really understand the concept of persuasive intent—that every aspect of an ad is selected to make a product appealing and to convince people to buy it." Such young children have yet to develop the skepticism of older children.

This exposure to advertising, critics claim, is effective. Juliet Schor (2004, 19) notes that by eighteen months children can recognize product logo's and before reaching their second birthday, they are asking for products by brand name. When they ask for a product they ask for particular brands:

> A 2001 Nickelodeon study found that the average ten year old has memorized 300 to 400 brands. Among eight to fourteen year olds, 92 percent of requests are brand specific, and 89% of kids agree that "when I find a brand I like, I tend to stick with it". (Schor, 25)

By the time a child is three and a half (Shor, 19) experts claim that children begin to believe that brands communicate their personal qualities, for example that they are "cool" or "with it." Children's social worlds are increasingly constructed around brands and the consumption of products has come to determine who is "in" and who is "out." Companies see babies as future consumers. This explains why companies target infants and toddlers by putting out items such as hats, shirts, and other clothing items with their logos on them.

Many critics of the marketing to children make a connection between marketing and consumption excess, whether it is the electronic media, drugs and alcohol or unhealthy food. In recent years health officials have become increasingly alarmed by the unhealthy diets and the increase in obesity among American children. Today

American children are among the most obese on the planet. According to Greg Critser (2003, 4) sixty one percent of Americans are overweight. And children are the most at "risk" for obesity. About twenty five percent of all Americans, Critser claims under the age of nineteen are overweight or obese. That statistic led the U.S. Surgeon General Dr. David Satcher to call obesity a national epidemic. "Today he noted," (qtd. in Critser, 4) "we see a nation of young people seriously at risk of starting out obese and dooming themselves to the difficult task of overcoming a tough illness." Media accounts of obesity point the finger at supersized portions and high caloric fast foods. Morgan Spurlock described the nature of MacDonald's foods and their metabolic effect in his documentary "Super Size Me." Food and beverages (Shor, 120) account for the largest segment of advertising dollars and are the most frequently advertised product in the media.

A number of recent studies have found an increase in the obesity among American children. According to the Centers for Disease Control(2004), since 1980 the proportion of overweight children ages 6-ll has more than doubled and the rate of obesity in overweight children has tripled. Today about 10% of 2-5 years olds and 15% of 6-19 year olds are overweight. Among children of color, the rates are even higher: 4 in 10 for Mexican and African American youth ages 6-19 are considered by the CDC overweight or at risk of being overweight.

Schor (34) notes that diets have gotten way out of line for most recommended nutritional standards. Many children are eating unhealthy foods. Children eat excessive quantities of advertised food products and not enough fruits and vegetables. "Among children aged six to twelve," she notes, " only 12 percent have a healthy diet and 13 percent eat a poor diet."

Although there are multiple contributors to the rise in childhood obesity, a reduction in physical education classes, an increase in the availability of snacks in the public schools and the trend toward supersizing food portions in restaurants, many researchers find a causal link with diet and the media. During this period in which childhood obesity has increased dramatically, there has been an explosion in media targeted to Children. And much of the media targeted to children is laden with elaborate advertising campaigns, many of which promote foods such as candy, soda, and snacks. It is estimated (Schor, 20) that a typical child sees about 40,000 ads a year on TV alone. Food advertising Schor argues is a major contributor to the eating habits of children noting (126) that over the last twenty years that the fraction of calories that come from snacks, rather than meals has risen thirty percent. Snacks tend to be nutritionally inferior to meals and thus contribute to an inferior diet.

Child development experts and media researchers have theorized that the media may contribute to childhood obesity in one or more of the following ways:

- The time using media displaces time they could spend in physical activities

- The food advertisements that children are exposed to on TV influence them to make unhealthy food choices.
- Children snack excessively while using media and they eat less healthy meals when eating in front of the TV
- Watching TV lowers children's metabolic rates
- Depiction of eating in the media encourages children to develop less healthy diets

Although the research is not conclusive a number of studies have found that the greater the amount of TV the greater the likelihood of obesity in children.

Decades of studies have shown that food marketing to children is effective. One of the earliest pieces of research that connected advertising to children was Marvin Goldberg's 1970 study of the differences between children who viewed television advertising and those who did not. He (Schor, 125) found that sugared cereals were more likely to be present in the homes of children who watched television advertising than those that did not. Other early studies (Schor, 125) have found that children between the ages of three and eight who watched television were more likely to request specific advertised products. Another early study found that children's media consumption was correlated with their body weight. William Deitz and Stephen Gortmaker in the journal *Pediatrics* (1993, 807-812) found in an analysis of data from a large national study of more than 13,000 children--the National Health Examination Survey--a significant association between the amount of time children spent watching television and the prevalence of obesity. The authors concluded that, among 12 to 17 year olds, the prevalence of obesity increased by 2% for each additional hour of television viewed after controlling for other variables. Indeed they (810) noted, "only prior obesity had a larger independent effect than television of the prevalence of obesity."

A 1994 study for the Centers of Disease Control examined exercise, television viewing, and the relationship to weight gain patterns for 4063 children between the ages of eight and fifteen. When grouped by age, sex, or ethnicity, exercise rates were inversely correlated with television viewed. Television viewing was also correlated with increasing body fat percentages. The study (Critzer, 73) found that the more TV a child watched the less the child exercised and the more likely the child was to be either overweight or obese. The CDC's 1999 Youth Risk Behavior Study (2002) which sampled more the 12,000 high school students nationwide, found that watching television more than 2 hours a day was related to being overweight.

It has also been noted by many social critics that alcohol and tobacco companies aim some of their advertisements at young people. A number of studies have found that children are watching a large number of alcohol ads in part because, as Schor notes, the programming "was more likely to be seen by youngsters than by adults." Analysis of ads such as Camel's Joe Camel ad and Budweiser's cute animal characters such as Spuds MacKenzie and the talking lizard campaign suggests that they have strong appeal to children. A 1998 study done by Kidcom (Schor, 133) found that the favorite commercial of kids aged six to seventeen was the Budweiser frog commercials. Another study found that more children ten to seventeen could identify the Bud-

weiser frogs than the Vice President of the United States. Children are also exposed to alcohol and tobacco in television programs, films and videos.

Media violence has also been seen to have deleterious effects on children. For decades various forms of violent entertainment have been viewed as having a pernicious influence on children. Concerns over the impact of media violence on children has existed long before the current uptick of violent television programming, "slasher" movies, and violent video games. Jeremiads against media violence accessible to children have been a part of the American cultural landscape for a long time. In the 1920's Anthony Comstock in *Traps for the Young*, warned of the effects of newspapers on children. In the 1950"s Frederick Wertham in his book *Seduction of the Innocent* warned that comic books led to juvenile delinquency and mental illness. Warnings of the pernicious effects on children watching television (Kirsh, 7) began in the late 1940's with editorialists raising the specter that watching television would lead to violent behavior and delinquency. In the early 1970's the U.S. Surgeon General warned of the negative influences of television on susceptible children. (Elkin and Handel, 1989).

A number of researchers have used different analytical tools to measure the amount of violence that children are exposed to on television, and to assess the impact of television violence on the aggressive behavior of children. Television by its content alone, some suggest, may teach children the ways of society. For example in studying the content of dramatic television George Gerbner found that "46 percent of all major characters commit violence and 55% suffer it."(qtd. in Elkin and Handel; 1989, 201). Kirsh notes that "Across the board, children's programming (i.e., programming aimed at children under 12 years of age) contains a constant barrage of violence." Gerbner also found that in 1967 a typical cartoon contained nearly three times as many acts of aggression as did the typical adult drama. (Gerbner, 1972) Recently, Kirsh (77) notes, Wilson, Smith, and colleagues found that 69% of all programs aimed at children 12 years of age or younger contained frequent acts of violence, with an average of 14 acts of violence per hour. Furthermore Kirsh found that certain subgenres of children's programming were likely to contain violence. He found that 100% of slapstick shows, 97% of superhero shows, 89% of adventure shows, and 48% of shows focusing on relationships depicted acts of aggression.

Even in watching commercials children are exposed to violence. Larson (2003) found that over one-third of some 900 commercials aimed at children contained aggressive elements. Studies show that the amount of violent content in dramatic and comedic programming viewed by children is far greater than the amount viewed in real life. Huston et. al. (1992) studied the viewing patterns of children and found that children will view more than 8,000 murders and 100,000 total acts of violence by the time they attend junior high school.

As users of a variety of entertainment media, children and adolescents are exposed to many forms of violence. Yet, knowing the amount of media consumption and the content of television programs and programming in itself does tell to what extent children are influenced. As Kirsh (211) has noted, more often than not levels of violent television consumption have been associated with higher levels of aggressive behavior." For example in an assessment of nearly 500 seventh and tenth graders McLeod, Atkin and Chaffee (1972) found a positive correlation between students viewing violent television programming and teenage self reports of aggressive behavior. In another study conducted by Slater, Henry, Swaim and Anderson (2003) the researchers found that among 6th and 7th grade adolescents, violent media use predicted both current levels of aggressive behavior, and also levels of aggressive behavior two years later.

There are numerous laboratory studies of the effects of violent programming on children. As Kirsch (169) notes most of these "laboratory experiments have found that violent cartoon exposure does, in fact, negatively influence preschool children." For example Loveass set up an experiment in which children viewed animation involving human like figures that hit and bit one another. These children chose to play aggressively with a toy, such as hitting a doll, as opposed to a nonaggressive toy such as a ball in a greater percentage than children seeing a nonviolent cartoon (Loveass, 1961). In his famous experiment Albert Bandura found that exposure to a violent cartoon resulted in greater aggression, such as hitting and kicking, towards a Bobo doll than the screening of a non violent cartoon.

Tannis Williams (1986) study of three Canadian towns, each with a different level of television exposure, found a significant relationship between the consumption of television programs and violence. Williams compared the levels of physical verbal aggressive behavior in children from three towns: Notel a town that had not received television prior the study, Unitel, which received one television station, and Multitel, a town that received four television stations. Williams sought to study the question of the effect of television on aggression by observing the children's behavior during free play and obtaining teacher and peer ratings of aggression for both Notel and the other two communities. Following the introduction of television into Notel, levels of physical and verbal aggression in Notel youth increased significantly beyond the levels before television was introduced. The children produced many more physical acts of aggression and verbal aggressive remarks two years after getting television than they had before. Williams concluded:

> ...there was a significant increase in the aggressive behavior of Notel children following the inception of television in the community. The increase occurred for both boys and girls; it occurred at more than one age level; it occurred for children who were initially low in aggressive behavior as well as those who were initially high in aggressive behavior, and it occurred for the same children studied longitudinally, and same-aged children compared cross-sectionally. (qtd. in Elkins and Handel, 199)

Williams' "natural experiment found that in various ways television had a significant impact on the violent behavior of children."

The media interest in children has come from several quarters. The media has publicized children with interesting story lines. Journalists and scholars like Jonathan Kozol, Henry Kempe, Juliet Schor, and Susan Linn have played key roles in drawing attention to the problems and causes of children. A wide range of problems affect children's lives such as poverty and divorce (Corsaro). Both the media and the academic establishment are increasingly interested in these problems and are drawn to these problems in increasing numbers. The issue of children, childhood, and the problems of children, once on the margin of both academia and the media, now as the above discussion suggests, is becoming a central concern of the media and of studies of the media.

PART II
The Transformation of the Child in Culture

CHAPTER FIVE
The Child In Utopia

Utopian thought presents an imaginative vision of the end at which social life aims. It is a form that has usually been the expression of dissent, a comparison of what is with what could be. However, utopian thought cannot be isolated from the mainstream of human speculation as a whole. The cultural, economic, and social factors which affect general outlooks, also influence and shape those outlooks which have been designated "utopian." And insofar as the idea of childhood constitutes an important theme in myth, literature, and political theory, it also plays a role in utopian thought. Childhood has attracted a great deal of attention in the recent past. Studies directed at childhood (Aries 1962; Zelizer 1985; Kuhn 1982) have investigated the historical development of childhood, the treatment of childhood in the past, the social value of childhood, and the literary treatment of childhood. The significance of childhood in literature, history, and sociology indicates that it is an archetypical theme embedded in social history. The significance of childhood in these areas raises the question of the existence and significance of the theme and conceptualization of childhood in utopian thought. The purpose of this chapter is to examine the status of childhood in utopian thought.

Students of utopian thought have examined a number of major themes in both utopian fiction and utopian discourse; technology, dystopia, pastoralism, socialism, the status of women, and family structure. However, conspicuously absent from such inquiries is an examination of the status of childhood, and the concept of childhood in utopian thought.[1] Utopia it would seem is for adults. At least, this has been the case it would seem in the utopian fiction and utopian proposals that comprise the standard works of each genre.

It is the argument of this chapter that many social theorists, particularly those writing since the advent of the industrial revolution, have found utopia to exist in a state of human development—childhood. Many of the authors cited here are not among the standard bearers of the utopian torch. But they have speculated on the nature of a better and more perfect existence, although sometimes in a digression, an aside, or a comment. The job of constructing this perspective involves piecing together casual references, tacit assumptions and common themes from the voluminous literature and commentary on modernity. These authors have found childhood to embody such simplicity, innocence, and virtue that they equate childhood with a utopian paradise. They suggest that social transformation rests on the ability of adults to recover, through the intellect and the imagination the mental set of the child, and the schemata within, which the child orders the elements of its experiences.

The logical starting point is the New Testament. "Except ye be converted and become as little children," Christ said, "ye shall not enter into the kingdom of heaven." (Matt. 18.3). Here, the child is seen as the herald of a new golden age. The New Testament establishes the traditional Christian role of the redemptive child. But for nearly four millennia (Aries, 1962) reverence for childhood remained only an undercurrent in Western thought. Under the shadow of original sin, children seemed closer to Satan than to "the kingdom of heaven." A utopian apotheosis of childhood did not emerge until the beginning of the nineteenth century.

At the beginning of the industrial revolution utopian writers looked to machines and to various forms of social organization—socialism, nationalism, as the foundation on which to establish a utopian society. However, some authors looked for utopia not in social foundation, but in a stage of human development—childhood. Childhood was seen as the "kingdom of heaven," a secular utopia centered around the nature of innocent and good beings. Recoiling from what they saw as the over civilized state of modern existence, they exalted the authentic experience of childhood as an end in itself. They embraced childhood as an exemplification of an alternative to the sterility of positivism and technology, urging that society affirm and accept childhood with all its potentialities. They encouraged the reception and reproduction of the experiences of childhood as a utopian model of existence.

At the beginning of the industrial revolution a cult of childhood developed in opposition to the features of industrialization, which saw the child as the embodiment of purity and innocence. Children came to be idealized for their special attributes; imagination, unselfconsciousness, and closeness to nature. There was a sense that modern life had grown dry, passionless, and hard, and that the regeneration of childhood was necessary. The Romantic Movement captured its sense of historical dislocation in the apotheosis of the innocence of childhood. A common strand of criticism of modern society was especially clear in numerous references to the ideal and utopian features of that earlier stage of human development—childhood.

In *Emile* Rousseau struck a note that was to be sounded again and again. "Love childhood," he (1964, 37) wrote, "indulge its games, its pleasures, and its lovable nature. Who has not looked back with regret on an age when laughter is always on the lips and when the spirit is always at peace." Rousseau held (1964, 68) that childhood has "its own way of seeing, thinking, and feeling, and nothing is more foolish than to try to substitute ours for theirs." Rousseau viewed the child as a personage living in a utopian state of nature, who was basically good until the forces of civilization corrupted their naive essence. Wordsworth also memorialized the pure nature of childhood. In his ode, "Intimations of Immortality for Recollections of Early Childhood," he observed that:

Heaven lies about us in our infancy!

Shades of the prison-house begin to close

Upon the Growing Boy (qtd. in Winn, 93)

Wordsworth expresses a combination of nostalgia for the past, and a longing for a new and transcendental future, found in the innocent characteristics of childhood.

Childhood provided Rousseau, Wordsworth, Blake, Lewis Carroll and innumerable others with both a haunting vocabulary of loss that could be exploited for social criticism of adulthood and modern industrial society, and an idyllic utopian existence. These authors juxtaposed a child's sincerity with adult artifice, the child's spontaneous feeling and intense experience with the utilitarian calculation of adults. The state of childhood was elevated to the status of a utopian ideal. The innocent child was a vision of psychic wholeness in a world where selfhood had become problematic and sincerity obsolete. Original sin was transformed into original innocence—the child was perfect and sufficient unto itself.

Among the twentieth century thinkers who have urged the regeneration of childhood in a technological society are several critical theorists. (See Chapter Two for a more complete discussion of the perspective of critical theorists on childhood.) One of the greatest costs of progress, critical theorists note, is the repression of memory—particularly childhood memory. "All reification," Theodore Adorno observed, "is forgetting: objects become thing-like at the moment when they are grasped without being present in all their parts, where something of them is forgotten" (qtd. in Schroyer, 191). The totality and wholeness that technological societies denied, critical theorists held, existed and could be sought in childhood, since children had not yet sensed the irreversible and ineluctable impoverishment which led to adulthood.

The hidden and utopian quality of lost childhood memories, their separation from the rest of life, their inaccessibility, and their incompatibility with conventional, purposeful, daily, activity, are described lucidly by Walter Benjamin. Benjamin, himself a collector of children's books appreciated the richness of experience to the child. Benjamin's writing on childhood, attempted to capture those moments of wonder, encapsulated in the simple gesture or the single action of a very young child. Benjamin believed that the child's grasp of his environment and the world around him went far beyond any discovery made in adult life. "For children," Benjamin (1973, 102) wrote:

> can accomplish the renewal of existence in a hundred unfailing ways. Among children, collecting is only one process of renewal; other processes are the painting of objects, the cutting out of figures; the application of decals--the whole range of childlike modes of acquisition, from touching things to giving them names.

To Benjamin, no Columbus, no Marco Polo had ever seen stranger and more fascinating and thoroughly absorbing sights than the child who learning to perceive, to taste, to smell, to touch, to see and use their body experienced. Benjamin idealized the child's capacity for unrepressed emotional and imaginative experience. In childhood, he found the self to be not only vigorous, but whole. Benjamin saw children as the incarnation of a miracle that awoke the sense of the marvelous not only in themselves, but in those who encountered them.

In Benjamin, the utopian impulse leads towards an apotheosis of simplicity and a fascination with the enchanted, the uncanny, and the inexplicable. He found these qualities in childhood and the fairy tales of childhood. He (1973, 102) took fairy tales so literally that he suggested that they made real fulfillment possible—particularly to children:

> The wisest thing—so the fairy tale taught mankind in olden times, and teaches children to this day—is to meet the forces of the mythical world with cunning and with high spirits...The liberating magic which the fairy tale has at its disposal does not bring nature into play in a mythical way, but points to its complicity with liberated man. A mature man feels this complicity only occasionally, that is when he is happy, but the child first meets it in fairy tales, and it makes him happy.

Benjamin was drawn to the sense of enchantment; the engagement with "liberating magic" that the child experiences in the fairy tale. He depicted the child's sense of knowing and understanding as transformative. For it is these history-making acts of the child he felt which invests everyday experience with consciousness and meaning.

As early as 1941 Max Horkheimer expressed a serious concern with the disappearance of childhood. Just as the presence of the child could be a cause for joy, so its loss could be a tragedy. "Development has ceased to exist," Horkheimer (1941, 381) wrote:

> The child is grown up as soon as he can walk. During the heyday of the family the father represented the authority of society to the child, and puberty was the inevitable conflict between these two. Today, however, the child stands face to face with society at once, and the conflict is decided even before it arises.

Horkheimer regarded this as unfortunate. The separation that the adult world imposed between reality and play and the demarcation of these activities into specific contexts was not part of the normal structure of childhood. He believed children did not view the world like that—at least not until they were taught to do so. In his (1941, 381) striking phrase, "The child, not the father, stands for reality." But in the technological era, a space where children could be at home in the world, where they could be the subject and not only the object of history, no longer existed.

In *Eclipse of Reason* Horkheimer searched for a liberated future through regaining the "mimetic impulse of the child." Imitation, Horkheimer argued, was one of the primary means of learning in early childhood. The whole body was an organ of mimetic expression in which such manners as laughing, crying and speaking were acquired. Eventually, however, civilization transcended the mimetic impulse in favor of rational, goal directed behavior:

> Conscious adaptation and, eventually, domination replace the various forms of mimesis. The progress of science is the theoretical manifestation of this change: the formula supplants the image, the calculating machine the ritual dances. (1977, 115)

Horkheimer, however, implied that mimesis need not be repressed; it could imitate life-affirming characteristics such as the sense of justice of the father and the instinctual love of the mother that were superseded by later civilization. The imitative impulse, Horkheimer (1977, 179) argued, could be restored through language:

> Language reflects the longings of the oppressed and the plight of nature; it releases the mimetic impulse. The transformation of this impulse into the universal medium of language rather than into destructive action means that potentially nihilistic energies work for reconciliation...Philosophy helps man to allay his fears by helping language fulfill its genuine mimetic function, its mission of mirroring the natural tendencies. Philosophy is at one with art in reflecting passion through language and thus transferring it to the sphere of experience and memory.

Ontogenetically Horkheimer maintained that this condition is present in the young child, it is only later tragically overcome by civilization and maturity.

For Horkheimer the child lived in open communication with the world, and the world in turn invited exploration from the child. Speech for children was not only an instrument of communication, but the very essence of their jubilant nature. Things in the world challenged the child, disclosed themselves to the child. Language comprised the mode through which the child realized himself. It was through language that the child restructured, invented, made history and transformed his given reality, for the transforming nature of language allowed the child to become fully realized as a human being. It was vital, Horkheimer felt, that the child be permitted to live this life-phase fully, to play and let things disclose themselves.

For Horkheimer language was the child's praxis on the adult world—and man's hope for an alternative to the deterministic laws of technological society. As long as the adult can recover through the intellect, the imagination or the involuntary memory, the mental set of the child, and appropriate for himself the schemata within which the child orders the elements of his experiences, then he can relieve the profound reality of his erstwhile condition, and can even retranslate it into terms comprehensible to other adults.

This apotheosis of childhood is stated in compelling form by Ernst Bloch. A student of utopian thought, Bloch argued that history was not subject to deterministic laws that left no place for humans and their dreaming. Bloch's vision of history culminated in nostalgia for the "homeland" seen in childhood, but lost to adulthood:

> The root of history is working, creating man, man who transforms and outstrips the conditions of his existence. Let him achieve self-comprehension and ground his life in real democracy, without renunciation and estrangement; then something will arise in the world that all men see in childhood, a place where no one has yet lived; homeland (qtd. In Wager, 333).

In the return to the lost world of childhood the love and security sacrificed by the catastrophe of growing up are recaptured. The more acute the suffering of the time of separation, the more keen the joy of returning home again.

Gunter Grass in *The Tin Drum (1959)* suggests such a return to a homeland orchestrated by a child able to evoke the language that Horkheimer described. As a newborn infant, Oskar, the narrator, is aware of the distance between child and adult and decides not to grow up. He remains in the body of a three year old child. Years later, Oskar, now a professional drummer in a cabaret, succeeds in bringing about communication between adult and child, and a return to childhood, for he has discovered the secret of evoking the language that Horkheimer searched for. Having forgotten all the routine pieces normally performed by and for adults in the cabaret, Oskar (445) begins to improvise: "...I did not play what I could, but what I knew from the depths of my heart. Oskar succeeded in pressing drumsticks into the fists of a once three year-old-Oskar...I revealed the world from the point of view of a three year old." The adults in the cabaret themselves have a childish vision of Oskar: they see him as the Pied Piper and are ready to follow him anywhere. And Oskar's drum playing gradually transforms them into children. They take each other by the hands and join in singing the children's songs that Oskar's drum playing inspires in them. Accompanying them on his drum, he (1959, 446) "led on the whole group, which was now shouting with glee, giggling and foolishly babbling with the voices of children." His success (1959, 447) is indisputable: "Every evening the guests all called for Oskar, for his tin drum, for the one person who was able to evoke the child of every patron, no matter how old he might be." The beholders of the child themselves become children, and are happy.

The recovery of childhood is a prominent theme in the countercultural critique of modern technological life in the late 1950's and 1960's. The distinction between "straight" and "hip" often divided generations. The notion was perhaps best epitomized in the Yippie slogan not to trust anyone over thirty. The association between the innocence of childhood and the romantic idea of childhood wisdom was explained by the fact that children had not yet had the opportunity to learn the terms by which an adult perspective is defined. One of the Movement's dominant themes entailed a devaluation of adulthood as a bad bargain with life in which one gave up more than one got. "I am never quite free of the forces attempting to make me grow up, sign contracts, get an agent, be a man." Raymond Mungo observed (1970, 136-137) in his memoir of the counterculture. "I have seen what happens to men. It is curious how helpless, pathetic, and cowardly is what adults call a Real Man...If that is what is manhood, no thank you."

Again and again countercultural authors and cult figures exalt childhood and childlike characteristics. Stanley Kubrick's 2001: A Space Odyssey, a cult film of the sixties, treats childhood with reverence, repect, and a sort of utopian nostalgia. One of the enduring images of 2001 is the cinematic offspring of the film's conclusion. After a mind-bending psychedelic voyage, the surviving astronaut of a journey to Jupiter finds himself confined to a luxurious apartment in which he ages and is transformed into a celestial starchild. In the last shot, the starchild hangs in space, contemplating Mother Earth beneath it. With its childlike luminescent eyes the starchild promises a radically transformed future. The starchild offers the prospect of an end to human destruction, and an innocent new beginning.

Many of the figures of the counterculture in the sixties discovered in the child the harbinger and the shape of a cultural revolution. Norman O. Brown urges (1972, 60) humanity "to regain the lost laughter of infancy." In *Slaughter House Five*, subtitled "The Children's Crusade," Kurt Vonnegut's hero Billy Pilgrim is a childlike figure who invents himself and his universe as a way of coping with the harsh reality of World War II. Norman Mailer found the saving quality of the hipster-psychopath's behavior in the retreat to childhood. Mailer noted that when the psychopath acted out his infantile fantasies, he was trying to go back to the early days of his life, which had determined his character and course ever since, and remake the decisions that led inexorably to the present. In his (1959, 320) attempt "to try to live the infantile fantasy the hipster-psychopath tries to reconnect with his childhood rather than trying to repress it. Theodore Roszak, who tried to capture the zeitgeist of the Movement in his book *The Making of a Conterculture*, extolled his readers (1975, 114) to recapture "our childish sense of the world enchanted." Instead of politicization as a means to perceptive self-consciousness and human emancipation he appealed to an increasing "adolescentation."

Though dissent during the sixties did not remain strictly theoretical, the period saw the emergence and popular reception of several authors whose works were deeply hostile to the dominant spirit of the age. Often, as noted above, they found alternative possibilities in the recovery of child-like forms of consciousness. Two theorists who rationalized this theme and gave it structure were Herbert Marcuse and Paul Goodman.

Herbert Marcuse attempted to redefine the social status of the child, transforming Original Sin into Original Innocence. Western society, Marcuse argued, had developed a concept of childhood which contained the dominant features of what he termed "the performance principle." However, Marcuse contended that childhood, along with art and fantasy contain the negation of "the performance principle." Childlike fantasy retained the structure and tendencies of the psyche prior to organization by reality. Thus, childhood linked the deepest layers of the unconscious with the products of consciousness; preserving the archetypes of liberation, the tabooed images of freedom. Childhood preserved the meaning of the subhistorical past; images of liberation are kept alive in literature, art, and in the imagination of children. "Historical possibility," Marcuse (1962, 145) held, is present in "childish fantasy."

To Marcuse, freedom from social conventions and utilitarian calculation made the child an emblem of a fuller, more sensuous and imaginative life and a focal point for a potentially sharp critique of modern society. In Marcuse's work, childhood remembrance becomes a decisive weapon in the struggle against domination. Domination is made possible, he suggests, because the "ability to forget" sustains submissiveness and renunciation. Such forgetfulness reproduces the conditions that produce injustice and enslavement. "Against this surrender to time," he (1962, 212) continued, "the restoration of remembrance to its rights, as a vehicle of liberation, is one of the noblest tasks of thought." Childhood represented remembrance, and is viewed as a vehicle for the liberation from the restraints of civilization. For Marcuse the nature of childhood had two distinct but related social uses. On the one hand, an exaltation of childishness pointed to a critique of technological society. Childhood presented a new reality with an order of its own. Childhood also provided a mechanism for a brief imaginary escape from technological society.

Paul Goodman was among the first strong voices to say that the problems of growing up in American society derived from the nature of society rather than the deviance of young people. "I assume," Goodman (1960, xvi) wrote, "that the young really need a more worthwhile world in order to grow up in at all." In *Growing Up Absurd* he described how the system "thwarted and insulted" the natural qualities of youth. In his later thinking on the subject Goodman added to the traditional romantic view of childhood as innocence or noble savagery the argument that helping to preserve what is best in the natural wildness of children involves adults as children; that is, it calls upon adults to reach for residues of their own childhood from which they may have only reluctantly "come down" into maturity. Goodman commended (1977, 143) the retrospective creation of adults who have sought to become like unto children, who can "draw upon child powers without inhibition." As long as the adult could recover the mental set of the child as appropriate for themselves, Goodman felt, that they could understand the profound reality of his condition.

Conclusion

The child has always been more or less central to human concerns. Curiously, little has been written about the significance of childhood in utopian thought. I have tried to show in this chapter that many writers who have contemplated utopia have used the child as a symbol for a liberated future. They have found that the child's very autonomy gives it a transformative power which influences not only the image we have of children, but also the image of the future. Children can be considered incomplete beings who in their very lack of completion, possess gifts that are lost in the finished product.

The writers described in these pages found a utopian condition not in the historical past or the historical future, and not in a particular place or in a pastoral or technological condition. They found utopia in a special point of human development—childhood. They contrast the riches of childhood experience, the child's great capacity for impressions and experience, with the poverty of mature adult perceptions of experience. They express a longing for lost innocence—the possibility of continuing to be childlike and pure in an increasingly corrupt and dominated world. The key to bliss is not science and learning, or any transcendence that man can store up in himself, but a childlike state of innocence. They hold that modern society can only achieve happiness by finding the garden of childhood once more. Utopia can be gained only by going back to the future.

NOTES

1.   It is probable that this absence reflects that in traditional utopian texts, both literary and philosophical little is said about the nature or the status of childhood. In utopian literature children do not figure prominently as characters. And in both conventional utopian literature and utopian thought discussions of childhood would seem to be largely absent. This inquiry examines the symbolic use of childhood in authors who speculate about the nature of a utopian society and a utopian existence, but not in utopian tracts.

CHAPTER SIX
The Child In
Contemporary Science Fiction Films

Recently there has been a proliferation of scholarship on the contemporary status of today's children that has pointed out the progression from the historical absence of childhood to the loss of childhood. Several significant social critics have held out the prospect that childhood is becoming an endangered species; that the industrial world at least, is entering a stage where childhood has ceased to exist. Everywhere one looks, these authors contend, it may be seen that the appearance and behavior of adults and children are becoming increasingly indistinguishable. These critics have, in compelling terminology, warned of the impending demise of childhood. David Elkind has described the emergence of what he calls "the hurried child," Marie Winn the phenomenon of "children without childhood," Neil Postman the "disappearance" of childhood, and Valerie Suransky the "erosion" of childhood. Collectively Elkind, Winn, Postman, and Suransky present evidence to support the claim that the charm, malleability, innocence, curiosity, spontaneity, and sense of wonder of children are currently being degraded and transmogrified into what they feel are the lesser features of pseudo-adulthood.

Neil Postman in particular contends that the major cause for the expulsion of childhood from modern society is the media which has promoted "the unseating of childhood through their form and content" (1982, 120). Children, he contends, "have virtually disappeared from the media" (1982, 122). And "when they are shown, they are depicted as miniature adults in the manner of thirteenth and fourteenth-century paintings"(1982, 122). On television and in films, Postman contends, children do not differ significantly in their interests, language, dress, behavior, and attitudes from adults.

It may well be that these contentions about the decline of childhood are correct, but one would search in vain to find evidence of these changes in recent American science fiction films. The direction of social transformation described by these social critics and the cultural transformation represented in contemporary science fiction films are seemingly at variance. Paradoxically, as the jeremiads describing the loss of childhood have become more shrill, the sentimental child (invariably a male child) is appearing as the idealized subject—a carrier of innocence and imagination—in a significant number of contemporary science fiction films. This chapter is about the profound transformation in the depiction of children in science fiction films from the nineteen fifties to the present decade. Over the last decade the image of children in science fiction films has changed dramatically in a way that is in sharp contradiction to the claims of social critics such as Postman and Elkind.

Any discussion of science fiction films must begin with an examination of the notion of science fiction itself. Although critics fail to agree on the precise meaning of the term, it may help if its significant components are identified. John Brosnon in his book *Future Tense: The Cinema of Science Fiction* notes that in the first place science fiction must involve science in some way. It is not fiction necessarily about science, but fiction that invariable uses science as a basis for extrapolation (1978, 9). In *Science Fiction in the Cinema* John Baxter noted that science fiction films are films which are not concerned with individuals, but with "movements and ideas" particularly the notion of "the threat of knowledge" (1978, 7–11). The films discussed below involve films that are concerned with the themes of knowledge, science, and society.

In contemporary science fiction films, children rather than being eliminated as Postman has suggested, are becoming increasingly prominent. The powerful figure of the child is becoming increasingly common. The nature of the child is being glorified and amplified in a way that is distinctive from the past. Rather than collapsing the distinctions between childhood and adulthood, in contemporary science fiction films the differences in the way that children and adults see and understand the world are being emphasized.[1] The motion picture industry has produced within the last decade scores of science fiction films in which children, or those who possess the sensibilities of children, are able to imagine and understand, what adults cannot. The abundance of these films no doubt is to some degree the result of commercial pressure. The majority of ticket purchasers are under twenty one. However, the variety of such films, and the force of their characterizations cannot be explained solely in terms of market forces. As Leslie Fiedler noted about the presence of children in another medium "So ubiquitous and symbolic a figure is, of course no mere reproduction of a fact of existence, he is a cultural invention, a production of the imagination" (1962, 219).

In any society, the ideas and images concerning the child emerge from their representations in works of art and coalesce into a dynamic pattern. By looking at these representations not only individually but as a coherent corpus, one can discern a distinctive motif. In looking at the representation of children in science fiction films of the last thirty years one can discern a change in the representation and idealization of the status of childhood.[2]

Freud called attention to "the peculiar amnesia which veils from most people (not from all) the first years of their childhood usually the first six or eight years" (1938, 581). It is this total forgetfulness of a near universally shared condition that Freud felt makes it so difficult, if not impossible to come to terms with the reality of childhood. Yet, despite the intensity of childhood experiences, Freud found memories of these experiences in later years to be fragmentary at best. Freud attributed this phenomena known to modern psychologists as "childhood amnesia" to the progressive repression of infantile sexuality.

Following up Freud's observations, but dissatisfied with his explanation of this massive failing of memory, Ernst Schachtel proposed the following explanation: In "modern western civilization" memory organizes past experiences in service of present needs, fears, and interests. Adult memory is organized into categories that are shaped by society. These categories, he asserted "are not suitable vehicles to receive and reproduce experiences of the quality and intensity typical of early childhood, because they are shaped by the biases, emphases, and taboos of adult culture." (1959, 288-289). Schachtel explored the dynamics of a cultural dichotomy between the phenomenon of "childhood amnesia" in which memory was essentially conventionalized so that memories which were incompatible with culture were forgotten, and the "recovery of forgotten (childhood) experience" in which the "hidden qualities of lost memories" were affirmed (1959, 290). This dichotomy is instructive in examining how the status of childhood in science fiction films has undergone a transformation from the fifties to the present.

Many of the science fiction films of the fifties reflect such a "childhood amnesia." In these films children are absent, inconsequential, and their view of the world is left unexamined. In contrast many of the science fiction films of the last decade have as their project the recovery, exploration, and apotheosis of childish ways of thinking. In many of the science fiction films of the last decade children are not only a more significant presence, their competence, virtue, and innocence are unquestioned. Between the nineteen fifties and the present, the image of children in science fiction films has been transformed; the images of children has shifted from forgotten objects to an object of sentiment.

One of the striking characteristics of fifties science fiction films is that children hardly exist in the social space of the film. They live in a world in which they are treated as the objects and not the subjects of activity. They live in a world in which history is made of them and for them. They reside in social space without directed intentionality, they constitute without praxis. This deficient awareness, this forgetfulness of the being of childhood is indicative of a far reaching "childhood amnesia" that permeates these films.

In many important science fiction films of the fifties children are simply not present. There are no boy pals for the robots and aliens in these films as there are in contemporary science fiction films. In *Forbidden Planet* (1956), Robby the Robot had no boy pal to hang out with like subsequent robots Artoo Deetoo in *Star Wars*, (1977) Jinx in *Spacecamp,* (1986) or Max in *Flight of the Navigator,* (1986). In these later films the robots act in loco parentis to the children in their care. They are in effect surrogate fathers to dependent children. In the science fiction films of the fifties when friendly aliens traveling in advanced spacecraft encountered earthlings, they encountered mature adults. The aliens of *It Came From Outer Space* (1953) encountered John Putnam, a nonconformist writer and astronomer. In *The Day the Earth Stood Still* (1951) Klaatu, the soft spoken visitor from the stars "goes among the people" and finds a friend in the fair minded, middle aged Helen Benson. Children are generally absent from the social landscape.

When present, children in these films are subordinate to adults, needing their help and protection. In *Them*, (1956) atomic testing has created giant mutated ants which threaten civilization. The film opens with a lone child—a sort of Job's Messenger— clutching a doll to her chest, stumbling out of the desert warning of "Them." The searchers discover smashed buildings and vehicles in the desert. As they finally trace the ants that have caused the destruction to a storm drain they find the ants with two children who are also caught in the nest. In the film's terrifying finale, Ben Peterson, a New Mexico state trooper, sacrifices himself to protect the children, helping them crawl to safety while the ants attack him.

Although children in these films warn of impending dangers, they are helpless to do much about it. Children who complained about relatives or neighbors acting strangely were mistrusted and powerless. In the opening sequence of *Invasion of the Body Snatchers* (1956) Dr. Miles Bennell tries to explain that an invasion has taken place. "For me," he says "it started last Thursday," and the film flashes back to Dr. Bennell, a country doctor returning home after a city visit. A small boy who runs down the road along which Dr. Bennell is driving claims that his mother "isn't my mother any more." Later a boy is brought into Dr. Bennell's office by his grandmother to explain that his mother "isn't real." But no one pays any attention until it is too late. Children themselves are ineffective at resistance. Later Dr. Bennell sees a man holding a pod ask his wife "Shall I put this in with the baby?" "Yes," she replies , "Then there'll be no more crying." The film insinuates that children are a nuisance—to humans and alien pod people. The troublesome children and their incessant crying are symbolically annihilated.

Invaders From Mars (1954) opens with little Jimmy looking out his window to see a flying saucer land. The aliens take over the minds of adults including his parents by inserting crystals into their brains. Little Jimmy chronologically behaves and thinks like a miniaturized adult. He is not irrational, hysterical, or subjective; he sees the world in factual and objective terms—the way men do—he goes to the authorities. After a struggle Jimmy convinces the army that aliens are indeed in residence under his house. In his close encounter Jimmy takes a journey from the insular self centered safety of childhood into the tricky territory of adult choice and responsibilities.

Science fiction films of the fifties not only rejected the child, but the childfied adult. Individuals who don't fit the advanced technological mold are viewed as children, as incomplete beings who haven't yet reached the age of maturity. The nature of the child evokes fear, especially for those whose existence is assured by an armature of reason. For them the irrationality which the child embodies is a threat. As the Martians tell the primitive earthlings in *Angry Red Planet* (1960), "You are technological adults, but spiritual and emotional infants." In *The Thing* (1951) Dr. Medford Carrington, is derided by the pragmatic journalist Henry for his intellectual naïveté. "He doesn't think like we do. These geniuses. They're like nine year old's playing with a new fire engine." These films suggest an antagonism between societal progress and childhood that is resolved in renouncing childhood. The experiences of childhood and the personality structure of childhood are seen to be insignificant and incompatible with progress.

In contrast, the films of the last decade depict children as the carriers of immutable values who possess imaginative and original ways of viewing the world. A growing number of science fiction films have idealized the child's capacity for unrepressed emotional and imaginative experience. In these films utopianism only exists within the souls of children, childlike creatures from beyond the stars, or childfied adults. The child is seen to possess as his or her birthright capacities for candor, understanding, curiosity, and spontaneity. In many of the science fiction films of the last decade the world in which children live has increasingly become a world in which children are the subjects rather than the objects of history. They are not only present in the social world—they act in it. This history making power of these children, the transforming nature of their actions upon the social world, arises from the praxis of individuals who are intentionally directed upon the world. And they participate and act in the world as children. Children play the traditional Christian role of redemptive child. These films are straightforward in their affirmation of the redemptive power of children. In them children manage to come up with original ways of viewing a world hardened, stratified, and over weaned by its own power. Maturity becomes less trustworthy, and childlike traits become more alluring. These films take delight in the child's way of seeing and experiencing the world. The innocent child is seen to be a vision of psychic wholeness, in a world where selfhood had become problematic.

Many of the most significant science fiction films of the last decade *2001: A Space Odyssey, (*1968) *Close Encounters of the Third Kind*, (1978) and *E.T. The Extraterrestrial* (1982) have treated childhood with reverence and respect. One of the enduring images of *2001* is the cinematic offspring of the film's conclusion. After a mind bending psychedelic voyage, the surviving astronaut of a journey to Jupiter finds himself confined to a luxurious apartment in which he ages and is transformed into a celestial starchild. In the last shot, the starchild hangs in space, contemplating Mother Earth beneath him. With its childlike luminescent eyes the starchild promises a radically transformed future. The star child offers the prospect of an end to human destruction, and an innocent new beginning.

In the films of Steven Speilberg the best people are those who retain a childlike receptivity to the unknown. Speilberg, a latter day catcher in sci-fi, perceives children as the bearers of eternal verities and immutable values.[3] In his films only those with childlike innocence are able to understand and comprehend modernity. All adults not informed by love and innocence are by implication inauthentic and sterile.

As the plot of *Close Encounters of the Third Kind* unfolds those with childlike sensibilities are able to form a rapport with the visitors from another world. The film establishes a two class system; the childlike and the non-childlike. Roy Neary, an electrical power company lineman, who enjoys tinkering with electric trains, a three year old boy, Barry, and an assortment of visionaries witness the lights of alien spaceships. They are as one character comments, the "invited guests." Lacombe, the official chasing the saucer sighting is a benign scientist of good will, with a seraphic smile— essentially a wise child, sympathetic to the child like dreamers, for he shares their instinctive trust of the aliens. As reviewer Jack Kroll noted, even the spaceships have a childlike quality. As the ships pass the city of Muncie, "a little red UFO comes skittering after the bigger ships," much like "the lost little dwarf or chipmunk stumbling after his dignified elders" in the old children's cartoons (1977, 92).

The first presence of the visitors is registered by a child's toy that is activated by their probe of the house. The child's toy celebrates this event by clapping it's cymbals together. Joy is reflected in Barry's face as he smiles delightedly at the whacky happenings taking place in his living room. It is the grown-up mother who is scared and apprehensive. Barry, in an hilarious scene circumvents his mother's anxiety as he chases the lights that have animated his toys out the door into the alien ship.

Many of those who encountered the alien ship are haunted by visions of a cone shaped object. The film follows the actions of Roy Neary and some of the other visionaries who are drawn to the spot where the aliens have chosen to meet the earthlings— Devil's Mountain Wyoming. When the alien ship lands a technician notes the childlike quality of the event; "It's trying to teach us a basic tonal vocabulary. It's the first day of school fellas." In the final scene the mothership disgorges a swarm of wide eyed space tykes. These small delicate, luminous space children with soulful, large eyes gaze at Roy with joy and wonder. And Roy returns their gaze with the starry eyed wonder of a child. With his kid's grin and childish gate, Roy gets into a line of steely, square jawed, sharp eyed astronauts who have been chosen to return with the aliens.

In Speilberg's *E.T. The Extraterrestrial* the dichotomy between the adult world and the world of childhood is starkly drawn. The elfish E.T. with drooping arms and roly-poly sawed off torso is left behind when his spacecraft abruptly takes off because of the possibility of being detected. As E.T. sees those who are pursuing his spacecraft the camera focuses on the keys jangling ominously, like a jingly ring of teeth from the waist on one of the pursuers. Marooned on earth E.T. is befriended by a young boy, Eliot, whose gentle innocent nature matches that of the ancient botanist from the stars, E.T's heartlight, a cosmic sensor of good and innocence senses that Eliot can be trusted.

Eliot protects E.T., fearing that the authorities will seize the miraculous creature and do things to him. Afraid that his mother would "do the right thing"—turn E.T. into the authorities—Eliot keeps E.T.'s presence a secret sharing it only with his brother Michael and his sister Gertie. Eliot explains to Gertie that she shouldn't tell their mother "Because-grown-ups can't see him. Only kids see him." His explanation is born out. On Halloween Elliot's mother fails to see E.T., even when she knocks him over. Like adults in general, she is too busy and preoccupied to see the enchantment before her. Eventually E.T's presence is threatened. Eliot sees government agents on the old fire road where E.T. was almost detected. There are people in the neighborhood who have never been there before. Eliot senses that the world of adults is closing in before E.T. can "phone home." The authorities are bugging Eliot's neighborhood. A van filled with audio snooping devices appears on the block. And the operator of the illuminated control panel has a large ring of jingling keys on his belt. Voices from the neighborhood are heard from the control panel.

When the authorities close in E.T. and Eliot are sick from cosmic loneliness. The intrusion of the authorities is jarring. Mary, Eliot's mother, opens the door and there is a faceless astronaut on the doorstep. She bolts for the window and a sheet of plastic comes over it. A man in a spacesuit tapes it to a frame. The house is quickly and efficiently converted into a gigantic airtight package, encapsulated in transparent vinyl, with huge air hoses climbing up over the roof and circling the structure.

Even when the intentions of adults are benevolent in adult terms, they are experienced by Eliot as threatening. Knowing that the authorities would seize his miraculous little creature and do things to him Eliot engineers an escape in which the children of the neighborhood collaborate. Eliot's relationship to E.T. poses a critique of the adult world, and suggests a nostalgia for lost innocence—the possibility of continuing to be young and pure in an increasingly scientifically corrupt and aging world: to be Eliot and convert the "Keys" poisoned by power and the quest for objective knowledge.

In the post-Speilberg era it has become *de rigueur* for children to be at the center of science fiction films. In *Spacecamp* (1986) a racially and ethnically mixed group of children become astronauts and fly and land a space shuttle. In *Explorers* (1986) 3 kids, a dreamer, a scientific wiz, and a kid from the wrong side of the street, receive instructions on how to build a spaceship in order to visit their teachers, who turn out to be spacekids who watched American television. In *Solarbabies* (1986) a group of orphaned children (on rollerskates) save a dry world from a water shortage imposed by an elite called the "Protectorate." In *Flight of the Navigator* (1986) twelve year old David, after falling into a ravine comes home to the nightmare of strangers living in his house and nobody knowing who he is. David escapes from NASA scientists who want to study his brain waves via a sleek saucer run by a friendly robot named Max. In one hilarious scene David stops the saucer at a filing station, and tells the attendant that he just wants to "phone home." Like David, many of these recent science fiction films attempt to return to and recover the lost innocence of childhood.[4] In these films the status of children shifts from original sin to original innocence. Children replace adults as the touchstone for morality.

The value of children in these recent films seems to be in sharp contradiction to the public and private value of children cited by recent critics. As noted earlier, critics, like Winn, Postman, and Elkind have argued that children are being rushed out too soon into adult-like behavior, clothing, language, entertainment, and sexual activity. Others argue that as a society American society is becoming increasingly hostile to children. This uneasiness is now being expressed in a variety of ways by several scholars and writers. In *Broken Promises* W. Norton Grubb and Marvin Lazerson argue that the sentimentalization of childhood has tended to stop at the family's own door step: "In contrast to the deep love we feel and express, in private, we lack any public love for children," (1982, 51–52) Some commentators have expressed alarm at the private decisions of increasing numbers of couples not to have children (1987, Wattenberg). Vance Packard (1983) has written about "endangered children" in "an anti-child culture." Germaine Greer without reservation asserts that modern society is "profoundly hostile to children" (1982, 2). Letty Pogrebin has asked "Do Americans hate children?" (1983, 47).

The transformation of the status of childhood in science fiction films suggests that there is a paradox between social reality and cultural idealization. At a time when the sentimental child is disappearing from society, he is appearing in the spotlight in science fiction films. Why the shift from the periphery to the center of art? How did the valuation of childhood change so dramatically within a relatively short period of time? In the recent films children seem to be used as a counter ideology to science and technology. The essential function of the child in these films is to symbolize the rejection of science and technology. Children are viewed as incomplete beings who in their very lack of completion possess gifts lost in the finished product. These films suggest the popular Rousseauian conception of the child as a personage living in a state of nature, basically good until the forces of civilization corrupt his naive essence. As science and scientists are portrayed as alienated from nature in such films as *Close Encounters of the Third Kind, 2001, E.T.*, and *Flight of the Navigator* the child is shown to be the incarnation of simplicity, naturalness, and innocence. The notion that a mere falling short of adulthood is seen as a guarantee of insight, innocence and wisdom. These films suggest a Pastoralism which finds a Golden Age, not in the advance of history and civilization, but in the beginning of each lifetime.

Although today many eminent social critics lament the passing of childhood, and some are disturbed by the adultification of the child in the media, the science fiction films of the last decade have taken delight in the innocence and emotional spontaneity of childhood. It is possible that these changes confirm Marshall McLuhan's observation that when a social artifact becomes obsolete, it is turned into an object of nostalgia and contemplation. However, the images of childhood that hold sway in these films are rooted in particular forms of ideology which have tended to elevate process over being, the inexplicable over the rational, childlike mentalities over adult understanding, and the uncorrupted child over a corruptible adulthood.

The contemporary science fiction film has revitalized romantic cultural modes, and presented an edge of dissent. They juxtapose the child's sincerity to the artifice of adult maturity. They apotheosize childhood, elevating becoming over being, and the process of experience over its goal or result. Familiar definitions of adulthood and maturity become less trustworthy to them, and childlike traits become more alluring. The innocent child becomes a vision of psychic and social wholeness in a world where the self has become problematic. At bottom they register a protest against industrial society, urging us to phone home.

NOTES

1.   This has not been the case in horror films where children regularly appear as evil and menacing. For example "The Exorcist," "The Omen," "Children of the Corn," "It's Alive," and "Village of the Damned."

2.   This chapter seeks to explore the ambiguous imagery that surrounds the modern consciousness of the idea of childhood in science fiction films. As Peter Briskind suggests, films have a frame of reference that they supply to an audience: "If we add up all that movies say and show about how we are supposed to be, we find that they present a 'world view,' an 'ideology,' that conveys an attitude toward everything from the trivial to the profound, from what we eat for breakfast to whether we should go to war. Even the most apparently innocent aspects of script and casting costumes, and camera angle, are charged with meaning. Stories are perhaps the most obvious carriers of value" (1983, 2–3).

3.   For those who do not remember, the title of Salinger's famous novel referred to his protagonist's fantasy of watching a group of children playing in a field of rye near the edge of a

cliff. When one of the children would fall over the edge of the cliff Salinger's hero would "catch" the child.

4.   Children have also become increasingly visible as emblematic innocents in music videos such as Sting's "Russians" where images of children are juxtaposed with stark images of bureaucrats, and Madonna's "Open Your Heart" where Madonna is rescued from her bondage to her fans and her own image by an innocent child. The innocence of childhood is also touched on in the increasingly frequent switcheroo movies like "Vice Versa," "Like Father Like Son," and "Big" where the films focus upon how (male) children react to being trapped in an adult in an adult body in a grown-up world. These films juxtapose the man-child to real adults.

CHAPTER SEVEN
The Symbolic Use
of Childhood in Popular Music

Many contemporary social critics, as noted in the previous chapter, argue that as a society American society is becoming increasingly hostile to children. Neil Postman (1982) in particular contends that the major cause for the expulsion of childhood from modern society is the media which has promoted "the unseating of childhood through their form and content" (1982,120). Children, he contends, "have virtually disappeared from the media" (1982, 122). And "when they are shown, they are depicted as miniature adults in the manner of thirteenth and fourteenth-century paintings" (1982, 122). In the mass media, Postman contends, children do not differ significantly in their interests, language, dress, behavior, and attitudes from adults. With few exceptions (Neustadter, 1989) most critics (Elkind 1981; Winn 1983) have accepted and elaborated this view of the eroding status of children in popular culture.

As a counterpoint to these descriptions of the disappearance of childhood there are contemporary descriptions of its joyful, pleasurable, and necessary aspects in popular music.[1] It may well be that these contentions about the decline of childhood are correct, but one would search in vain to find evidence of these changes in American popular music over the last two decades. In popular culture the direction of social transformation and cultural transformation are seemingly at variance. Paradoxically, as the jeremiads describing the loss of childhood have become shriller, the sentimental child is appearing as the idealized subject-- carrier of innocence and imagination—in a significant number of popular songs. Over the last decade the symbol of childhood and the image of children in popular music stands in sharp contradiction to the claims of social critics such as Postman and Elkind. Where once the sentimental child and childhood were absent in what Greil Marcus called "the musical culture," the sentimental child and childhood are now important and consistent themes in contemporary popular music.

In contemporary popular music over the last two decades children and childhood, rather than being eliminated as Postman has suggested, are becoming increasingly prominent. In many songs the powerful figure of the child is becoming increasingly common and symbolic. These songs glorify childhood, and amplify its unique virtues. The abundance of such songs no doubt is to some degree the result of commercial pressure. The majority of record purchasers (Frith, 1981) are under 21. However, the variety of such songs, and the force of their characterizations cannot be explained solely in terms of market forces. As Leslie Fiedler (1982, 219) noted about the presence of children in another medium "So ubiquitous and symbolic a figure is, of course no mere reproduction of a fact of existence, he is a cultural invention, a production of the imagination."

In any society, the ideas and images concerning the child emerge from their representations in works of art and coalesce into a dynamic pattern. By looking at these representations not only individually, but as a coherent corpus, one can discern a distinctive motif. It is of course difficult and hazardous to generalize about a subject as wide and diverse as themes in popular music. In the years before the last two decades popular music dealt with themes such as sex, money, and death. It still does. When children appeared they appeared primarily in novelty songs such as "All I Want For Christmas Is My Two Front Teeth" and "I Saw Mommy Kissing Santa Claus." Much as in the past that Philippe Aries described, children are absent. A widespread apotheosis of childhood in popular songs awaited the last two decades when cultural developments promoted a sense that childhood might be endangered. During this period there has been a key shift in the attitudes toward childhood in popular music. A cult of childhood has developed linking antinomianism with romantic primitivism using the symbol of the child for uncorrupted innocence and simplicity.

The Transformation of the Status of Childhood in Popular Music

In the early sixties (1962) Peter Yarrow wrote, and Peter, Paul and Mary recorded "Puff the Magic Dragon," a compellingly melancholy song about the inevitability of growing up and losing a vision of childhood. The song appeared at about the time such critics as Postman and Elkind date the disappearance of childhood. The song begins by describing Puff the Magic Dragon who "lived by the sea and frolicked in the autumn mists in land called Honalee." It tells the story of Little Jackie Paper who loved that rascal Puff "and brought him strings and sealing wax and other fancy stuff." Their relationship is playful and their time together an idyllic adventure: The song describes how they travel with Jackie as a lookout perched on the dragons tail, encountering kings, princes, and pirate ships. At the conclusion of the song little Jackie Paper grows up and no longer frolics with his magical friend.

> A dragon lives forever, but not so little boys
> Painted wings and giant springs make way for other toys
> One grey night it happened Jackie Paper came no more
> And Puff that mighty dragon he ceased his fearless roar

Seemingly, Jackie Paper came no more because he, unlike Peter Pan, grew up and had no place in his life for magic and fantasy. It is not clear what happened to Jackie Paper. The consequences for Puff are clear; Puff no longer went to play along the cherry lane "so Puff that mighty dragon sadly slipped into his cave."

"Puff the Magic Dragon" nostalgically describes the loss of childhood. In "Puff the Magic Dragon" adulthood assumed an aura of inevitability. Protest took the form of elegiac regret. However, during the last twenty years many significant popular songs have revisited Puff's cave, glorifying childhood, using childhood as a symbol of innocence and purity, and urging listeners to cultivate childlike qualities. Popular songs have used childhood to critique adult society, described the plight of threatened children and sentimentalized the idea and status of childhood.

Rock is the music of the young. Sociologists often describe rock as "the music of youth." Rock has always glorified childhood and been suspicious of adulthood. The Coasters noted the pointlessness of adult knowledge. Adults usually command and babble, "Bring in the dog and take out the cat." Adult order means "yakety yak." "Hope I die before I get old," the Who sing on their classic, "My Generation." "As we get older and stop making sense," the Talking Heads observed on their *Speaking in Tongues* album. John Mellencamp states the case in "Jack and Diane," "Hold onto sixteen as long as you can." Adulthood is a form of deprivation; "Life goes on long after the thrill of living is gone." The person who has lived the most is not the one who has counted the most years, but the one who has felt life the most. Adults are identified by their insensitivity to the instinctive knowledge of youth. Growing up is not only hard to do, it is unfortunate.

Rock lyrics are suffused with the language of emotion and intuition. Logic and reason are everywhere associated with the loss of childhood and the death of vitality. In Supertramp's "The Logical Song" the power of the logical mind is equated with cynicism. The alternative to magical youth is cynical adult intellectualism. In youth, life is experienced as "wonderful," "beautiful," and "magical."

But then they sent me away to teach me how to be sensible,
Logical, responsible, practical
And they showed me a world where I could be so dependable,
Clinical, intellectual, cynical

Education mutilates instinct, killing intuition and an innocent appreciation of life, encapsulating all understanding in reason.

Given contemporary rock's commitment to instinct and authenticity, its hostility to education as a corrupter of childhood flows naturally. Paul Simon observes that "When I think of all the crap I learned in high school it's a wonder I can think at all." In "The Wall" Pink Floyd gives voice to teenage angst when they cry "Hey, teacher, leave those kids alone!" School is just another "brick in the wall." Rock itself claims to teach better than the academy. In "No surrender" Bruce Springsteen cries that "We learned more from a three-minute record, boy, than we ever learned in school." Alice Cooper exults that "School is out forever." A convention in rock is that wisdom is fostered not by formal education, but by its abolition. Youth, it is often insinuated, knows well intuitively, whereas school mutilates perception.

In "Pets" Porno for Pyros simply proclaim that "Children are innocent." In "The Obvious Child" Paul Simon juxtaposes the taken for granted understanding of the world with the vision of the child. The song describes how some people see only the taken-for-granted objective world.

Some people say the sky is just a sky
But I say why
Why deny the obvious child?
Why deny the obvious child?

The song suggests that children know what adults "deny." The standard of knowledge is necessarily personal and subjective. There is in the child a kind of simplicity, an appreciation of the uncanny and the inexplicable. Something other than reason is the measure of knowing. A lie is not just a lie and the sky is not "just a sky." Rationality is secondary to emotion. Simon demotes rational empirical knowledge to a subordinate way of knowing and elevates the child's way of knowing as the fundamental way of knowing. The simplicity and innocence of childhood, Simon suggests, is often divinest sense.

Often in popular music the child's innocence is juxtaposed against the adult's artifice. The Jefferson Starship contrast the innocence of childhood and the hope of childhood with the corruption of American technological society in their (Hugo Award winning) concept album "Blows Against the Empire" (1970). The songs on the album describe the high jacking of a spaceship in order to "wave goodbye to Amerika" and "Say hello to the garden." It is a garden of children's delights compared to the artificiality and destructiveness of technological society. The lyrics juxtapose the child's sincerity against the adult's artifice. After "Hey Dick," in which Dick Nixon is advised that "there's a new world a-comin" the hope of that new world is epitomized on a song "The Baby Tree" a whimsical song about where babies come from:

> There's an island way out in the sea
> Where the babies they all grow on trees
> And it's jolly good fun
> To swing in the sun

Such babies are innocent, pure, and desirable, at least those that smile. The lyrics say that the adults will come, but they will not take with them babies that cry. The Starship presents a picture of the eternal awe and wonderment of a childhood Eden on a detemporalized bucolic island. But even here adults impose artificial distinctions based on appearances.

The need to escape Amerika and the artifice that adults have constructed becomes imperative in "A child is Coming." With the immanence of a birth, the prospective parents are confronted with a problem. The innocent child is threatened by the political imperatives of society.

> What you gonna do when Uncle Samuel comes around
> Askin' for the young one's name
> And lookin' for the print of his hand for the files in their numbers game
> I don't want his chance for freedom to ever be that slim
> Let's not tell 'em about him

The Starship shares the Christian admiration for childlike innocence, and adds a primitivist stress on the child's capacity for spontaneous feeling and intense experience. To the Starship freedom from social convention and utilitarian calculation make the child an emblem of a fuller sensuous and imaginative life, and a focal point for a sharp critique of modern society.

During the 1980's and the early 1990's threats to children came under intense scrutiny: there was widespread concern about child abuse, incest, molestation, and missing children (Best, 1990). The new interest in child victims came from several quarters. At this time a number of popular songs addressed the problem of child abuse. Suzanne Vega's haunting song 'Luka" described child abuse from the perspective of an abused child, exploring the emotional and psychological effects of abuse. The mawkish "Dear Mr. Jesus" features the voice of a young boy who is beaten by both his mother and his father begging Jesus to protect the children; "Please don't let them hurt your children, won't you keep us safe and warm." "What's the Matter Here" on the 10,000 Maniacs' *In My Tribe* album describes the outrage of a silent witness to the abuse of a neighbor child; "I hear them every day. Threats like: 'If you don't mind I will beat your behind." 'Slap you, slap you silly." Made me say O, what's the matter here? I'm tired to the excuses everybody uses, he's your kid, do as you see fit, but get this through that I don't approve of what you did to your own flesh and blood." In "Janie Got a Gun" Aerosmith describes the revenge of a teenager on her abusive father.

A number of contemporary hit songs and their accompanying videos deal with, and draw attention to, the alienation of children from family and society. These songs rarely present the social problems of adolescence as products of a flawed social system. The emphasis is on individual problems--troubled interpersonal relationships or insensitive individuals. Many of the songs use an emotionally riveting grabber. Horrific examples give a sense of the problems' frightening and harmful dimensions. In "Jeremy" Pearl Jam describes an archetypical lonely child ignored by busy and preoccupied parents. Jeremy lives in an imaginative world "drawing pictures...of mountaintops...with him on top." But, "Daddy didn't give attention Mommy didn't care." The violent consequences of parental inattention are described in the first person voice of an anonymous adult:

> clearly I remember...picking on the boy...seemed a harmless little fuck...but we unleashed a lion...gnashed his teeth, but the recess ladies breast...how could I forget...he hit me with a surprise left my jaw left hurtin...dropped wide open...Daddy didn't give affection...and the boy was something that Mommy wouldn't wear.

The consequences of parental neglect in the song are ambiguous. In the video Jeremy runs to school and commits suicide before his horrified classmates.

On their *America's Least Wanted* album Ugly kid Joe covers Harry Chapin's confessional "Cat's in the Cradle," a song which describes family separation and growing up with an absent father preoccupied with work:

> but there were planes to catch
> and bills to pay
> he learned to walk
> while I was away

The father is absent after his child's tenth birthday because he "has a lot to do." The tension of the relationship is conveyed through the father/son dialogue in which the son asks his father when is he is coming home. The father replies that he doesn't know when, but they will have a good time. The song ruefully develops the dramatic contrast between benign neglect and children's needs for significant others. The ironic result is that soon the son becomes "just like me" an absent father for his children, and too preoccupied to see his father. In "Cat's in the Cradle" definitions of maturity become less trustworthy, and childlike traits become more alluring.

Soul Asylum's haunting "Runaway Train" tells the story of a teenage runaway unable to cope with an unhappy past." The song describes the state of mind of a runaway in the first person:

> So tired that I couldn't even sleep
> So many secrets I couldn't keep
> Promised myself I wouldn't weep
> One more promise I couldn't keep

It describes the desperation, hopelessness, and mentality of the runaway. The song uses the image of a runaway train to describe the plight and condition of runaway children. It describes the hopelessness, and the mental condition of the runaways. For the runaways there is no permanence, they are "neither here nor there." There is no "coming back" and only disjunction and alienation to look forward to.

The song's straightforward description of the pain of growing up leads to an implicit critique of the dominant culture. The video opens with the message that there are "One Million Youths Lost in America." It uses the evocative pictures of missing children to typify and personalize the issue.

Hammer's platinum and Grammy-winning album *Please Hammer Don't Hurt Em* contains the following dedication in its liner notes:

> Who will be hurt? Those who do not value the life of a helpless child. The cold hearted killer who pushes the ten-year old into the streets to work rocks (crack), hop (heroin) and any other drug knowing what the end has in store for the innocent child. I'm going to hurt you until you understand that the children are our future and deserve to live. I find no fault in the children. I love them and I will help them. Help the Children.

He finds "no fault in the children." They are the model for a life of spirituality. Children are used as symbols of a saving trust.

The album itself contains the song "Help the Children," which is not only a rap warning to those who pose a threat to children, but a plea for the protection of children, inner city children in particular. The song's chorus asks the question:

> Will you let them be?
> Will you help the children live to see?

There are, the song maintains, children who are at risk:

> A generation's dying

Oh, how we're dying

The song describes several vignettes from black city life; a young girl with a child who has gone to an early grave; a mother by the phone waiting to hear from "another brother who has left his home"; and neighborhood crack sellers—"a dime back of crack the end of you"; racism, "black and white a constant fight"; and concludes that "many people die before they're twenty years old." These children know the miseries of urban life. They represent the hope of adults, like Hammer who see in the child the possibility for the fulfillment of their own dreams. Thus, Hammer concludes: "I've got to stand. To make a better way for a young black man. And land where the people smile. Been holding back for such a long while." The chorus urges listeners to "Help the Children."

If childhood is the source of goodness, than the trick is never to relinquish childhood and to protect childhood. The images of childhood in such songs as "Jeremy," "Cat's in the Cradle," "Runaway Train," and "Help the Children" are a new and important chapter in American child saving. These songs view children as priceless, lovable, vulnerable innocents to be cherished and protected for their own sakes.

Allied to popular music's insistence on the vulnerability of children is the sentimentalization of childhood. There is a significant trend to find a new valiancy and sentimental value in childhood. Crosby, Stills, Nash, and Young's "Teach Your Children" makes a plea to protect those of "tender years" "from the fears that your elders grew by." Children are seen as uncorrupted, good, and loving:

Don't you ever ask them why
If they told you, you would cry
So just look at them and sigh
And know they love you

Even though utilitarian adulthood is not inevitable, only teaching children well will avoid a recapitulation of the past that includes "your father's hell."

The consciousness raising and fund raising song "We Are the World" (1986) inspired by USA For Africa, combines rock's pantheism with the sentimentality of childhood. Michael Jackson, and a plethora of stars sang a catchy tune:

We Are the World
We Are the Children
We Are the Ones to Make a Better Day

The lyrics don't convey any specific information about poverty, but they sentimentalize the child, equating the future with childhood. It uses the symbol of the child to help encourage wanting to make "a better day" and a better world. In the accompanying video to the song, which consists largely of the stars singing portions of the song, this response is elicited through close-ups of starving African children.

Jackson's "Heal the World" begins with a child's voice with playground noises in the background making pleas that the current generation look out for their children and their children's children. The video montage is a multicultural series of children's faces. In his memoir, *Moonwalk*, he noted and explained his sentimental view of children writing that "They aren't jaded. They get excited by things we've forgotten to get excited about anymore." "The magic, the wonder, the mystery and the innocence of a child's heart," he has said, "are the seeds of creativity that will heal the world."

In Whitney Houston's "The Greatest Love of All" (1985) the protection, cultivation, and respect of children and childhood innocence is urged:

I believe the children are our future
teach them well and let them lead the way
Show them all the beauty they possess inside
Let the children's laughter
remind us how we used to be

The song accords a special place to children. It suggests that there are other values besides the shopping mall and the corporation, values which are embodied in the "beauty" children possess, and their "laughter" which is held to be a means for the recovery of an earlier and purer self.

The song's message "No matter what they take from me, they can't take away my dignity" stems from the referential equation of childhood with innocence, sincerity, and love. Something, it is insinuated, that should not be lost in adulthood--something an ominous "they" cannot take away. It expresses the ideal of a society of service rather than dominance. In the song's view, children, because they are untainted by social artifice, embody the moral innocence and emotional spontaneity which seem absent from the public realm. And true greatness, is in a life of service that extends to the caring of children.

White Lion's (1991) hit "When the Children Cry" uses childhood as a position from which to criticize the world of adulthood, and as a model of utopian freedom. The song begins with a regretful explanation to a child of the mess grown-ups have made of the world, how utilitarian calculation and adult artifice have lead to an "evil world" of senseless destruction: "Where man is killing man and no one knows just why?" It is the perversity of adults that is the problem, not that of children. The song jars its audience into realizing that growing up is too often a process of narrowing self interest, leading to selfishness and aggression. Children, it is insinuated, have an advantage in spiritual matters because they have not yet been consumed by such concerns. The chorus juxtaposes Original Sin with Original Innocence; the uncorrupted nature of the child with the fallen nature of adults, suggesting a terrestrial childhood paradise which anticipates the eternal one in which "the new world begins."

The song echoes the New Testament, "Except ye be converted and become as little children, ye shall not enter the kingdom of heaven" (Matt. 18:3). Freedom from adult faults makes the child the symbol of utopian possibilities.

> Little child you must show the way
> To a better day for all the young
> Cause you were born for the world to see
> That we all can live with love and peace.

The lyrics echo the sentiments of Romantic writers such as Blake, Wordsworth, and Rousseau, that children because--they are untainted by adult artifice and rationality--embody moral innocence and emotional spontaneity making it possible to live in peace without war and hostility to one another.

Eric Clapton's beautiful Grammy award-winning ballad "Tears in Heaven" also deals with childhood as an object of sentiment. The song is sung to a child, asking validation from the child: "Would you know my name if I saw you in heaven." Whereas the child belongs in heaven, the singer notes that "I must be strong and carry on 'cause I know I don't belong here in heaven.." The song deals with the death of an innocent child. (Clapton's young son fell to his death from a window in a tragic accident.) In the song the death of a child is formalized into an act of public mourning. The song and its popularity indicate that child death provokes not only parental sorrow but social bereavement as well.

In 10,000 Maniacs' "These are Days" childhood takes the form of psychic wholeness, a simple, genuine self in a world where selfhood has become problematic and sincerity seems obsolete. The image of childhood provides a focus for nostalgia and a remembered past of innocence and wonder:

> These are days you'll remember. Never before and never since, I promise, will the whole world be as warm as this. And as you feel it, you'll know it's true that you are blessed and lucky.

The childhood self is not only made whole but vigorous. Childhood is described as "blessed," "lucky," and "touched" by something wondrous and these are "days you'll remember." Admiration for childish mentality is joined with fascination of the child's capacity for unrepressed emotional and imaginative experience. These days are filled with laughter. We know the universe first and always by feeling. Feeling is strongest in youth. In youth people are most fully themselves. At bottom, "These Are Days" registers a protest against the moral innocence and emotional spontaneity which seem absent from the public realm.

Children have also become increasingly visible as emblematic innocents in music videos not explicitly about childhood, such as Sting's "Russians" where images of children are juxtaposed with stark images of bureaucrats and military officials, and Madonna's "Open Your Heart," where Madonna is rescued from her metaphorical bondage to her fans and her own image by an innocent child. In the video for Bette Midler's Grammy award winning song, "From a Distance" (1990) pictures of a tribe of children poignantly illuminates the song's message of the senselessness of war.

Conclusion

Contemporary popular music celebrates childhood and youth and its attendant innocence and goodness. It denies rationality, equating reason and adulthood with the death of the spirit, and looks for the apotheosis of the self in the purity of childhood instinct. There is the sense in popular music that modern life has grown dry and passionless, and that one must try to regenerate a lost intensity of feeling and sense of wonder and innocence. Among those who express this sentiment there is a common strand of antimodernism and nostalgia made clear in numerous references to children, childishness, and images of children.

The songs cited in this chapter amplify themes that were espoused in the literary cult of childhood that coalesced in the 19th century. Childhood provided Rousseau, Wordsworth, Blake, Lewis Carroll and innumerable others (Lurie, 1990) with a haunting vocabulary of loss that could be exploited for social criticism of adulthood and modern society. They were convinced that the "progress" of their day was headed in the wrong direction and that society needed to recapture a childlike vitality. Popular music, like the earlier writings of the Romantics juxtaposes the child's sincerity against the adult's artifice, insinuating the idea of the uncorrupted child. To Wordsworth, Blake, Rousseau, White Lion, 10,000 Maniacs, Hammer, et al., freedom from social convention and utilitarian calculation make the child an emblem of a fuller sensuous and imaginative life--a focal point for a potentially sharp critique of modern society.

The value of childhood in these recent popular songs is in sharp contradiction to the public and private value of children cited by recent critics. This valuation is found in different genres of popular music, easy listening (Huston), rock (the Starship), rap (Hammer), and Heavy Metal (Ugly Kid Joe). The transformation of the status of childhood in popular music suggests that there is a paradox between social reality and cultural idealization. At the same time when the sentimental child is disappearing from society, he or she is appearing in the spotlight of some important popular music. Why this shift from obscurity to the center of art? How did the valuation of childhood change so dramatically within a relatively short period of time? In recent popular music children seem to be used as a counter to the failures of the modern world; war, fam-

ine, materialism, political oppression, and drugs. The essential function of the child in
these songs is to symbolize the rejection of such aspects of modern life. Children are
viewed as incomplete beings who in their very lack of completion possess gifts lost in
the finished product. They suggest the popular Rousseauian conception of the child as
a personage living in a state of nature, basically good until the forces of civilization
corrupt his naive essence. These songs suggest a pastoralism that finds a Golden Age,
not in the advance of history and civilization, but in the beginning of each lifetime.

These songs recommend and even celebrate daydreaming, playing, singing, and
refusing to grow up. They overturn adult pretensions, and make fun of adult institutions, including school, social security numbers, and the military. They mock current
assumptions and practices and embrace an imaginative, unconventional, and noncom-
mercial view of the world. They appeal to the imaginative, questioning, rebellious
child within the listener, acting as a force for change. They support the rights of a disadvantaged section of the population--children against the world of grown-ups and
submit childishness as a utopian model, that in recovering childhood, human beings
would become like angels.

Although today many eminent social critics lament the passing of childhood, and
some are disturbed by the adultification of the child in the media, some significant
popular music of the last two decades has taken delight in the innocence and the emotional spontaneity of childhood. It is possible that these changes confirm Marshall
McLuhan's observation that when a social artifact becomes obsolete, it is turned into
an object of nostalgia and contemplation. However, the images of childhood that hold
sway in the songs considered in this examination are rooted in particular forms of ideology that have tended to elevate process over being, the inexplicable over the rational,
childlike mentalities over adult understanding, and the uncorrupted child over corruptible adulthood. In these songs the symbol of the child has two distinct but related
social uses. On one hand, an exaltation of childhood points to a critique of adult conventions; on the other hand, it provides adults with an imaginary escape from such
conventions.

These contemporary songs have revitalized romantic cultural modes, and presented an edge of dissent. They apotheosize childhood, elevating becoming over being, and the process of experience over its goal or result. Familiar definitions of adulthood and maturity become less trustworthy, and childlike traits become more alluring.
The innocent child becomes a vision of psychic and social wholeness in a world
where the self has become problematic. At bottom they register a protest against
modern society, urging Jackie Paper and the rest of us to visit again Puff's magic cave.

NOTES

1.   The term popular music here is used here follows the description of Simon Frith. Frith (1981,6) makes the distinction between music that is produced with no reference to a mass market and music 'that is inseparable from the mass market in its conception...Pop music is created with the record industry's pursuit of a large audience in mind; other music is not." The term popular music is used here as a general term to describe the various different genres; rock, easy listening, and rap which reach large audiences and sell large numbers of records.

CHAPTER EIGHT
The Child in the Contemporary Memoir

Mary Gordon (1996, xiv) wrote in her memoir of her father that "I am primarily a writer of fiction, but I knew I couldn't present him as a fictional character because the details of his life, presented as fiction, would be too bizarre to be believed." Years ago people who thought they had a story to tell about their lives sat down to write a memoir, a story told directly from life, rather than a story fashioned by the imagination out of life. Many contemporary memoirs are written by novelists, who no longer find it necessary to shroud the events of their lives in supposedly purely imaginative works (Gordon, 1996; Harrison, 1997) Fiction demands that the writer invent; memoir exploits the gift of lived experience. Where once the novel based on the author's lived and remembered experience was the form chosen, the memoir has become the form for conveying that experience.

One of the attractions of contemporary memoirs is that they not only "show" and "tell," but they reflect on the process of telling itself. In many contemporary memoirs, the author successfully combines the techniques of fiction with essay writing, the personal with public dimensions of experience, and the documentary account with poetic and evocative recreations of experience. For many writers today, the memoir is the format of first, not last resort. American publishing is, in the words of Vivian Gornick (1996) experiencing a "memoir boom." The current age seems to be characterized by a need to testify about the meaning and significance of one's life.

Today, particularly in American culture, the memoir has become a popular choice for telling a story. "Alice B Toklas did hers and now everybody will do theirs," Gertrude Stein observed in *Everybody's Autobiography* (1973), referring to her companion, whom she impersonated in *The Autobiography of Alice B. Toklas* (1933). Contemporary times, it has frequently been noted (Atlas, 1996; Blais, 1997 Gornick, 1996), are characterized by a deluge of memoirs. Memoir seems to have become the fin-de-siècle literary form. The literary genre of memoir has become a particularly robust trend in contemporary American publishing. There has been a proliferation of titles, a noticeable presence on best seller-lists, special sections in book reviews and special sections in bookstores. No doubt commercial interests are involved in the proliferation of memoirs; many memoirs have been huge successes that authors and publishing houses would wish to repeat.

Not only are people moved to write their life stories, but there is a ready audience for the stories. Readers crave to know the live experiences of others. The popularity of memoirs for the book-buying public has been noted by numerous cultural observers. Blois (1997, 80) notes that "You would have to be living in a cultural vacuum not to have noticed that memoir as a genre is hot." James Atlas observed in *The New York Times Magazine* (1996) that the triumph of memoir is "now established fact." The memoir, Patricia Hampl asserts (1997), "has become the signature genre of the age."

Since the publication of Augustine's and Rousseau's confessions, the memoir has been a staple of a written form that involves the writer as self publicist, discloser, and author of personal history as against public history. Memoirs were once written by famous people, eminences basking in the twilight of their fame. They were the preserves of ex-presidents, public officials and celebrities. That has now changed. Today it seems that ordinary women and men are rising up to tell their story of how an individual life has meaning. Autographical writing, as Richard Coe (1984, 41) has observed, "is an assertion of uniqueness." The writer, by fixing his or her experience on the printed page, is making the claim that his or her life experience is of significance. The uniqueness of this experience mandates the telling of that experience.

In recent decades, there has been a notable flowering of narratives about the remembrance of personal pasts. A growing number of authors have a story to tell, a lesson to teach, a life to be made public. This new trend in confessional writing has produced a library of historical, sociological, psychological and cultural revelation. Memoirists witness their traumatic illnesses, racial experiences, sexual identities and family dysfunctions. It seems that there is no topic that is taboo, or not written about. The contemporary memoir has opened up a new kind of narrative authority for ethnic subcultures, for different sexual persuasions; for anyone, in short, whose experiences fall outside the themes of worldly success, power and moral spiritual growth, which were once prominent in American Autobiography.

This chapter is an attempt to identify and analyze a specific segment of this popular form of autobiographical writing—the memoir of childhood, which given the volume of such works, could well be considered a distinctive literary genre in itself. In *Mystery and Manners*, Flannery O'Connor (1969) wrote that "Anybody who has survived his childhood has enough information about life to last him the rest of his days." The sheer volume of contemporary memoirs on childhoods would seem to verify Flannery O'Connor's claim.

The task set here is to illuminate the memories of childhood in the contemporary memoir and cast some light on the kind of childhood that is remembered. This chapter asks: "what are the common and recurrent characteristics of childhood, as interpreted in the perspective of contemporary memoirs?" The ideas and images concerning the child emerge from their representations and coalesce into a dynamic pattern. By looking at these representations not individually, but as a coherent corpus, we can discern a system with its own images and landscape. The multiplicity of contemporary memoirs in which childhood is represented, varied as they are, forms a complex system with various levels of significance. By analyzing certain specific themes and images in the memoir, it may be possible to make visible some of the themes of a composite language that is the retrospective creation of adults who have written about their childhoods, a childhood they try to make sense of and bear witness to.

In general, memoirs that deal with childhood may be divided into two broad categories. In one are those works whose central purpose is to recapture the essence of a lost past. The means of achieving this end are diverse and various memoirists employ differing techniques to reach it. Frank McCourt and Mary Karr attempt a rigorous use of memory, whereas Mary Gordon's reconstruction is based at least partially on documentation of family and personal records. The second category contains those works in which the construction of a childhood world is not an end in itself but a pretext. Such recollections may serve as an outlet for the nostalgia of the adult for a long lost paradise that is believed to have once existed. The child in his or her own Garden of Eden is the vision offered by Jill Kerr Conway, Doris Kearns Goodwin and Elizabeth Spencer. Whatever the tools employed, these practitioners of memoir subscribe to the proposition that childhood is a central element in existence. In both of these perspectives, the childhood universe is usually portrayed as an extreme one.

This chapter is intended as an examination of the kinds of childhoods that are remembered, and of the types of childhood experiences that are recreated in literary form by contemporary men and women describing and examining the existence of their former selves. Memories and recollections of childhood may look at many facets of childhood, psychological and self-development, personality, religious faith, philosophical quests and political ideologies. There are, no doubt, many possibilities for dividing, organizing and classifying an inquiry into the myriad of memoirs that focus on and describe childhoods. There are many archetypical life scripts in memoirs of childhood.

The structure of this chapter is simple and topological in classifying and describing these archetypical life scripts. In many recent memoirs, there are elemental motifs of childhood that are discernible. The memoirs considered here conjure up, by way of symbols, images, and impressions, a picture of childhood with a pattern and significance that can be retrospectively interpreted. The recollections and descriptions of the unique landscape of childhood are myriad, comprising both a heaven and hell and in some cases a transitional space—a sort of purgatory that is neither a hell nor a heaven, by a transitional landscape betwixt and between. The archetypes of heaven and hell have been used by Kuhn (1982) to analyze depictions of childhood in fiction, and by Coe (1984) to examine childhood in autobiographical writing. In this chapter, this typology is applied to contemporary memoirs. The category of a purgatory, of childhood lived betwixt and between cultural borders, reflects the experience of childhoods in multicultural societies. They reflect neither experience of a hell or a heaven, but a childhood lived in often ambiguous and confusing space. This chapter will examine examples of each of these three depictions of childhood in the memoir.

The Hell of Childhood in Memoir

Children in the novels of Dickens and Zola for example are often the subjects of unbearable conditions and exploitation. The vision of childhood as a period of unmitigated suffering is by no means any longer unique to fiction. The aspects of life experience now appearing in memoir would in the past be addressed only in fiction. The social taboos on discussing violence, parental cruelty and incest no longer censor what appears in memoir. In recent memoirs, the source of suffering is not social and political turmoil, but sources closer to home. The story of inadequate and dysfunctional families has become one of the central motifs of the late twentieth century. Many children experience family break-up, fatherlessness, a parent's alcoholism, and physical and sexual abuse. For many grown ups, an unhappy childhood leaves an indelible imprint in memory. As Richard Coe (1984, 68) has noted, in his study of over 600 examples of autobiographical writing on childhood, there is a "high proportion of unhappiness" in childhood autobiography. Memoirists of unhappy childhoods fill books with descriptions of remembered miseries.

The catalogue of writers whose childhoods were miserable and intolerable is large and growing. The vision of childhood as a period of unmitigated suffering appears frequently in a number of contemporary memoirs. Every happening, every relationship and every event is framed by remembered unhappiness. The theme of the child as the victim of interfamily conflicts, whose home life is transformed into a domestic hell by the cruelty or neglect of parents is a recurrent one. The essence of a childhood perverted by the indifferent malice of authoritarian and capricious parents has been distilled in several contemporary memoirs. These memoirs describe children who experience terrible childhoods, which involve dysfunctional families, troubled parents, poverty and abuse. Lack of love, the interdiction of communication and physical cruelty are the elements that make up the infernos to which they are condemned.

There are numerous accounts of bad childhoods. In *Angela's Ashes* (1996) the story of Frank McCourt's Limerick childhood in the 1930's and 1940's McCourt begins his memoir by wondering how he survived:

> When I look back on my childhood, I wonder how I survived at all. It was, of course a miserable childhood: the happy childhood is hardly worth your while. Worse than the miserable childhood is the miserable Irish childhood, and worse yet is the miserable Irish Catholic childhood. People everywhere brag and whimper about the woes of their early years, but nothing can compare to the Irish version: the poverty; the shiftless, loquacious alcoholic father; the pious defeated mother moaning by the fire; pompous priests; bullying schoolmasters; the English, and the terrible things they did to us for eight hundred long years (199, 11).

The major tragedies of his "miserable childhood" (which is described with innocence, humor, and love of language) were his father's alcoholism and myriad childhood deaths.

Frank's father Malachy drank the family into semi-starvation and his wife into beggardom. Frank describes forays into the pub to try to bring his father home before he drank up all his weekly paycheck.

> When the farm money is gone he rolls home singing and crying over Ireland and his dead children, mostly about Ireland. If he sings Roddy McCorley, it means he had only the price of a pint or two. If he sings Kevin Barry, it means he had good day, that he is now falling down drunk and ready to get us out of bed, line us up and make us promise to die fore Ireland (1996, 95).

Malachy drinks not only the dole money, but a relatives "telegram money" for a new baby. "It's bad enough to drink the dole or the wages," Frank writes (186), "but a man that drinks the money for a new baby is gone beyond the beyond as my mother would say."

Almost as relentless as the father's drinking is the list of childhood deaths. Three of Frank's siblings die. The twins Eugene and Oliver die. A sister Margaret dies when she is seven weeks old. Later on Angela had a stillbirth, and then later still bore two more sons who did not survive.

Frank became ill with typhoid fever and was hospitalized on a fever ward for several months. The ward was empty, except for a young girl, Patricia, with diphtheria and "something else" who hemorrhaged to death. They are forbidden to talk to one another, laugh, or sing. But she loans him a book with the first works of Shakespeare he has ever heard. When the nurses learn Patricia is teaching Frank poetry, they transfer him upstairs to the end of a large empty ward. Soon after the separation she dies.

Two of Frank's boyhood friends, Mickey Spellacy and "Quasimodo" die of consumption. McCourt describes his first sexual experience with a consumptive young girl (Theresa Carmody) and describes how he was terrified that this had hastened her death.

The book is full of detailed descriptions of poverty. The overall impression of Limerick is dampness and misery:

> From October to April the walls o Limerick glistened with the damp. Clothes never dried: tweed and woolen coats housed living things, sometimes sprouted mysterious vegetations. In pubs, steam rose from damp bodies and garments to be inhaled with cigarette and pipe smoke laced with the sale fumes of stout and whiskey and tinged with the odor of piss wafting in from the outdoor jakes where many a man puked up his weeks wages (1996, 12).

The family home is next to the public toilet where residents of the entire lane disposed of their waste. A sadistic teacher peels an apple in front of his starving pupils, occasionally throwing them pieces.

Frank steals food from drunks. As the family becomes poorer Frank licks greasy newspapers for substance:

> ...I take the greasy newspaper from the floor. I lick the front page, which is all advertisements for films and dances in the city. I lick the headlines. I lick the great attacks of Patton and Montgomery in France and Germany. I lick the war in the Pacific. I lick the obituaries and the sad memorial poems, the sports pages, the market prices of eggs butter and bacon. I suck the paper till there isn't a smidgen of grease. (1996, 296)

Frank spots his mother in a crowd outside a priests house begging for any food left over from the priests dinner; "This is my own mother, begging. This is worse than the dole...It's the worst kind of shame, almost as bad as begging on the streets where the tinkers hold up their scabby children." 1996, 250) Frank becomes further alienated from his mother when he realizes that she is sleeping with their landlord to survive. Finally there is the terrible irony of World War II, that English factories were hiring Irish laborers, and this was economic salvation for many Irish families

In *The Liars Club* (1995) Mary Karr locates herself in the center of a chaotic world of alcoholic parents, a mother with a nervous condition, divorce, step parents, and their lovers whose relations to one another are constantly changing. Karr narrates with great force and wit the story of needy children and wayward parents and the awfulness of Leechfield, the town in which she grew up. Karr describes how she and her elder sister Leicia grew up during the 1960's in "a swamphole, a suckhole, and the anus of the planet," Leechfield in East Texas. "The oil refineries and chemical plants," Karr writes:

> gave the whole place a rotten-egg smell…Plus the place was in a swamp, so whatever industrial poisons got pumped into the sky just seemed to sink down and thicken in the heat. I later learned that Leechfield at the time was the manufacturing site for Agent Orange, which surprised me not one bit. That morning, when I woke up lying under the back slant of the windshield, the world smelled not unlike a wicked fart in a closed room…In the fields of gator grass, you could see the ghostly outline of oil rigs bucking in slow motion. They always reminded of rodeo riders, or of some huge servant creatures rising up and bowing down to nothing in particular (1996, 34–35).

Children play by chasing the DDT truck to see who will upchuck first. The beach is covered with grunge, rotting shrimp and man o war jellyfish. Karr's mother Charlie is stranded in this hell hole with two kids, a crazy mother dying of cancer, and an alcoholic husband. Karr describes a southern gothic horror story of a dysfunctional family. The book is replete with violence and alcoholism—both parents drank heavily and fought bitterly, moving from verbal abuse to physical combat with their daughters as witnesses, neglect, the tragic story of her mother who lost the children of an early marriage, stolen from her by a mother in law who thought she was incapable of raising them, her father's stroke, an aunt dying of cancer, and an episode of rape at age seven; "Think of two good-sized Smithfield hams—that's roughly how big I was. Then think of a newly erect teenaged boy on top of that and pumping between my legs." (1995, 68)

The central problem that haunts her life is her mother's "nervousness," an east Texas euphemism for bouts of insanity. Her mother becomes increasingly psychotic making a confused attempt on her daughter's lives, is adjudged "nervous" and removed to an institution. Karr describes her mother's breakdown in the voice of a lonely child observer watching her world fall apart:

> …exactly what led to Mother's near fatal attack of Nervous. Maybe drinking caused Mother to go crazy, or maybe the craziness was just sort of standing in line to happen and the drinking actually staved in off a while. All I know is that first Mother was drinking, then she and Daddy were fighting worse than ever, and finally they were hauling her away in leather four point restraints (1995, 125).

The essence of a childhood perverted by the malice of authoritarian and abusive parents has been distilled in the memoirs of Ruthie Bolton and Richard Rhoads. The story of Ruthie Bolton (a pseudonym) in *GAL (1994)* is told to the novelist Josephine Humphreys "the way that Southern stories are best told: out loud teller to the listener." (forward). The resulting memoir describes a troubled "unloved childhood" in a "no love family" and its transcendence.

Ruthie Bolton was born in 1961 to a 13 year old mother in an unpaved section of Charleston called Hungry Neck. She recalls that "They called me Gal, but of one time I

wandered past the yard and my grandfather hollered 'Get that gal out of the street.'"
After Ruthie's vituperative step-grandfather, Clovis Fleetwood beat Gal's young
mother for her promiscuity, she ran away abandoning Gal to him and his wife. The
mother that Ruthie never knew would be murdered by a lover who tied her to a bed
and set her afire. Her grandmother was bludgeoned by her husband who suspected her
of infidelity with a garden hose beyond recovery in front of the children.

After his wife's death Fleetwood subjects Ruthie and her sisters to a life of drudg-
ery, intimidation, humiliation and enslavement. Fleetwood commanded them to scrub
the house "spick and span"and to serve him as if they were his handmaidens. After his
nightly bath he would order Gal to scrape the dead skin off the soles of his feet with a
knife. Later, describing the insect collection of her son, Gal notes (1994, 264) "I never
had anything like that, no hobby. Hobby! Your hobby was to get your ass up, get your
work done, that's what your hobby was!" While Fleetwood spent his money on girl-
friends and drink. The girls wore socks on their hands instead of gloves and ate
scraps.

The girls especially Ruthie are tyrannized and beaten. Ruthie described (267)
how "I wasn't getting nothing but beaten. I was beaten for socks. Shoes. Hair. Bump.
Any little thing." After the principal of her school tells Fleetwood that Gal has been
stealing lunch money he brutally beats her with a tree limb:

> He started beating me and beating me and beating me. I was jumping up all over the
> table. I was screaming. I was screaming, I was screaming, screaming and screaming.
> "Down the window, Daddy, please down the window so the neighbors don't hear."
>   He said, "The neighbors! I don't care about no neighbors! I'll up them win-
> dows. Open up them damn door! Open up them doors. You don't want the
> neighbors to hear? I want the neighbors to hear."
> And he beat me. He beat me. He beat me, he beat me, he beat me. He hit me so
> much that he happened to his own self, and when did that he went berserk. Then
> he took off his belt. I'm going to make water come out of your eyes he said
>   He didn't chop me with the leather end of the belt. He hit me with the buckle
> part. He had just chop and chop me and chop me. I was screaming and yelling but I
> never did cry. Never did cry. Never did cry (1994, 49).

After she escapes Fleetwood's brutality by moving out she embarks on a course of
promiscuity and drug abuse, endures a violent marriage, loses custody of her first child
before finding transcendence and sanctuary with a tender man and his family; "That
family changed my life. I came out of a no-love family, and fell into a love family"
(1994, 201).

The dismal hell in which Ruthie spends her youth can be considered the prototype
of those subsequently portrayed with variations in numerous contemporary memoirs
such as David Peltzer's *The Story of It* (1995) and *The Lost Boy* (1997). The essence
of a childhood perverted by the malice of an authoritarian and capricious parent has

been distilled in Richard Rhoades' *A Hole in the World*. The first sentence sets the stage and tone of Rhodes' childhood memoir. "When I was thirteen months old my mother killed herself." This awful fact is the "hole in the world" that defined and destroyed the author's childhood. After several itinerant years his father finally landed Rhodes and his brother Stanley in the house of a women who became their step mother.

Rhodes describes his step mother unambiguously as a ghastly sadistic monster and his father as "cowardly" man who allowed the step mother's abuse to go on until they were removed by the juvenile court. Rhodes uses political terms to describe what happened to him during the two years he lived with his step mother. He describes (1990, 88) his "victimization" "in the concentration camp of our stepmother years." "She tinkered sadistically," Rhodes wrote "with control worked out on the surface and the interior of our bodies."

Rhodes described (117) a tortured existence in which the stepmother imposed as rigid system of rules regarding how toilet paper was to be installed which were enforced "with violence" that included "slapping us, kicking us, bashing our heads with a broom handle or a mop or the stiletto heel of a shoe, slashing our backs and the backs of our legs with the buckle of a belt."

"Our stepmother" Rhodes writes (1990, 117) "tinkered more radically with manipulating what we took into our bodies and what we expelled." Rhodes describes a tortured existence in which he and his brother were systematically starved. Rhodes describes how he and his brother ate black eyed peas and hard boiled eggs "while she and Dad dined on pork chops and even steak, the meaty sear of their frying drifting back onto the sleeping porch to tantalize us…our cheeks gushed saliva." Both brothers are significantly under weight for their years and turn to scavenging.

In an horrific passage Rhodes describes how his stepmother attempted not only to control behavior and diet but bodily functions as well. Since the bathroom was near her bed room she forbade the brothers to use the bathroom at night. Rhodes graphically describes his struggle to retain urine:

> Dutifully I went to the bathroom just before climbing to my upper bunk on the north wall of the sleeping porch, but as soon as Stanley turned out the light and we settled down to sleep I felt my bladder fill. I lay awake then for hours. I tried to redirect my thoughts, tell myself stories, recite numbers, count sheep. I clamped my sphincters until they cramped and burned. Lying on my back, hurting and urgent, I cried silently to the ceiling low overhead tears running down my face without consolation, only reminding me of the other flow of body fluid that my commandant had blocked. When clamping my sphincters no longer worked I pinched my penis to red pain (119).

Rhodes urinates into a jar at night and surreptitiously empties it to avoid the wrath of his stepmother. The boy becomes an object to be used, misused, and abused when his cost outweighs his usefulness.

Richard Beredzen the former President of American University tells the story of a male incest survivor in his memoir *Come Here* (1993). In the first episode of the book Berendzen describes how when he was eight the "sexual abuse of my childhood began" when his mother summoned him into the bedroom while she was having sex with his father. The abuse will become a recurrent one. Although sex with both parents never recurred Beredzen describes how his mother became obsessed with him; his clothes, his academic achievement, and in disciplining him. The incest resumed when he was twelve. During the next three years he became the (1993, 7) "passion and her prey" of a woman whose mental instability took the form of repeated incestuous assaults on a child who was powerless to resist. In the darkroom and in the middle bedroom the abuse was repeated:

> Come here.
> It was in the afternoon, always in the afternoon, that my mother called me into the middle bedroom…
> I stopped and felt overwhelming stillness, the silence that negotiates between the living and the dead. The predator had found its prey…
> Even in the dim light, I always could see her eyes. Charged with a ferocious hunger, that eye followed me as I took off my clothes and hung them in the closet. My nakedness embarrassed me, her eyes contaminated me even before she touched me. Instinctively I knew this was wrong. That what my mother demanded was evil (1993, 20–22).

The episodes created "feelings of confusion, disgust, and terror slamming into each other, toppled by momentary convulsions of nausea, excitement and shame…confusion and torment" (21). Beredzen goes on to argue that his later compulsion to make obscene phone calls while he was president of American University originated in these incidents of childhood sexual abuse.

If we look at these memoirs as a group, some archetypal fairy-tale qualities are present in them. These are bleak tales of needy children. Each narrative recounts memories of inadequate nurturing, the fear of an evil step parent. Every happening, every event, is seen through the prism of remembered misery. And yet despite the abuses they endure each of these memorists displays an inner toughness that enables them to survive mental manipulation and torture. In general, the narrators not only lived to tell about their unhappy childhoods, they prosper. They are redemptive children. Their voices are purer than the voices in the world and the adults they encounter. The children in these memoirs are resurrected as adults. These memoirists' emerge from their childhood hell, if not unscathed, intact into a world of mature satisfaction.

The Heaven of Childhood in Memoir

At the other end of the scale, are childhoods that are visions of a paradise lost. Memories of an idyllic childhood are not as numerous as those of miserable childhoods. In his study of autobiographical writing on what he called "the Childhood," Richard Coe (1984, 62) noted that of the 600-odd examples in his study a sentimental "nostalgia is rare." Perhaps because of the focus on abuse and dysfunctionality in memoirs, some memoirists are inspired by the desire to recapture something of a paradise that has been lost or partially lost, forever. As counterparts to the depictions of infernal horrors of childhood, there are the descriptions of its more joyful aspects. As can be expected the latter only rarely measure up to the former. Bliss is harder to communicate than suffering, and the many attempts to recreate a childhood paradise all too often result in uncomfortably sentimental effusions characterized by a mawkish enthusiasm for nature.

Jill Kerr Conway probably comes closest to capturing the eternal awe and wonderment of a childhood Eden. In Conway's memoir *The Road from Coorain* (1990) Conway tells her story of growing up on an isolated sheep farm in the Australian outback.   Joyful scenes of children frolicking in Edenic landscapes are lyrically described; "Magpies used to perch on the windmill's stand and sing every morning at first light. This sound would mingle in waking with the early morning smell of flowers in the garden. It was an idyllic world" (1990, 51).

Conway's description of her childhood is literally a childhood in the garden. Conway's Coorain (1990, 31) was a "delightful place to live,"...a terrestrial paradise. In simplest terms Conway describes her childhood in a tropical garden of Eden. After a rain:

> The transformation of the countryside was magical. As far as the eye could see wild flowers exploded into bloom. Each breeze would waft their pollen round the house, making it seem as though we lived in an enormous garden...Bulrushes shot up beside the watercourses, and suddenly there were waterfowl round about, erupting into flight as one approached...Evidences of the fertility of the soil were all about us (1990, 33). Soon I would drift off to sleep in the evening bathed in the perfume of stocks, wallflowers, and heliotrope in the summer, the crisp aroma of chrysanthemums in autumn. A whole bed was given over to Parma violets, and great fistfuls of them would sit in the middle of the roundtable on which we dined in summer on the southern screened veranda (1990, 41).

Perhaps the account is tinted in brighter colors than reality might justify. Yet, this Edenic garden in the outback provides a refuge from civilization in which Conway and her two brothers grow up in an uncorrupted state of nature

Conway's joyful existence is based on an acceptance of her family's interdependence with a bountiful nature. Conway's social world is as bountiful as the natural
world that she describes. Her parents are "jubilant" with their lives, full of plans for
the future. She "worships" her brothers who are gentle and generous (1990, 34), her
mother "encouraged a strict equality between us." Even after the brothers go off to
boarding school Conway's loneliness is moderated by a "fascinating new companion,"
a kindly hired hand who was a source of knowledge and friendship. Coorain is the
perfect setting for conversation, security, and happiness. Parents, siblings and friends
make for a harmonious prospering community.

The advent of a radiant future promised in earlier passages is threatened by the intrusion of events. After an eight year drought, her father's death, her older brother's
death, the family moves to the city where Conway prospers. However, what grows in
the plains of New South Wales she optimistically and metaphorically notes "hugs the
earth firmly with its extended system of roots about which the plant life is delicate but
determined"(1990, 23).

In Doris Kearns Goodwin's *Wait Till Next Year* (1997) the 1949–1957 Brooklyn
Dodgers are the gateway through which Goodwin recollects memories not only of
baseball, but of family, neighborhood, community, and the sensibilities of girlhood.
Her early years are happily governed by family, neighborhood, and the baseball calendar. *Wait Till Next Year* is an old fashioned reminiscence, an elegant, endlessly affectionate evocation of a vanished way of life. The childhood paradise regained through
the memory of baseball is a sublime one, a rich lode from which the most precious
metals can be extracted. Baseball has been very good to the young Doris Kearns.
Baseball is her tie to many relationships, "a lasting bond had been forged among by
father, baseball, and me." (1997, 13). The neighborhood too is both divided and
united by their love of baseball.

At the center of her childhood is the "invisible community of baseball," (1997,
42) a community which reached across generations and social class. The butchers at
the Bryn Mawr Meat Market were Giant fans; "They would mock my Dodgers, I
would pretend to be angry, but the truth was I loved going into their shop..." (1997,
63). The Lubar's and Bartha's were ferverent followers of the Yankees. "We carried
on our arguments on the street, in the corner stores, and in each other's homes. If no
minds were changed, we took great pleasure in our endless debates and our shared
love of the sport." Even her first confession is received by "a baseball loving priest"
who commends her "with a chuckle, 'say a special prayer for the Dodgers'" (1997,
108).

Her childhood has it's own the Dodgers and Doris highlight film. After Roy
Campanella addresses a church meeting Doris meets the Dodger catcher noting that
"The warmth of that broad smile was all I needed to know that this was a night I would
never forget" (96). Gil Hodges eloquently accepts her St. Christopher medal as a gift,

and her autograph encounter with Jackie Robinson gives "an unexpected moment I would treasure for the rest of my life" (1997, 202).

The Dodgers shine so brightly that her childhood glows. Television she observes "was only another wonder in a world of constantly unfolding wonders, like the stories my mother told me, the first book I read, or my first trip to Ebbets Field" (1997, 120). Through her mother Goodwin came to worship the world of books. Every night her mother comes to read to her. She loved listening to her voice, so much softer and less piercing than her own. The block is an "extended family:"

> Unlike more affluent modern suburbs, whose fenced homes are encircled by large ornamental lawns, the houses on my block were clustered so close to one another that they function almost as a single home. We felt free to dash in to any house for a snack from the mother-in-residence, race through the side door in search of playmates…(1997, 57).

The family vacationed at Jones Beach "which remains the finest beach I have ever see…A paradise for children and grown ups alike" (1997, 40). The nuclear family, with the idyllic setting of Brooklyn constitutes the framework of an undisturbed and undisturbing paradise.

Goodwin portrays a state that is the essence of simplicity, but at the same time extraordinarily complex. The Eden of childhood gives way to a more mature realization of the fifties. It is a romantic tabulation within a realistic framework. Goodwin describes a time when her life seemed idyllic, but also remembered are fears of polio, air raid drills, the Rosenburg executions, and McCarthy. If there were, she says, such worries that "hung over our childhood days like low-lying clouds" (1997, 10) they hung over a field of dreams.

Elizabeth Spencer's *Landscapes of the Heart* (1996) is a loving evocation of a beloved lost world. The Carrollton Mississippi into which she is born is a comfortable, well-to-do island of relative prosperity set on green hills above the Mississippi Delta. Spencer's childhood seems to have been an enchanted Eden of Watermelon cuttings, swimming holes, the lengthening shadows of pecan trees, and long horseback rides along sleepy dusty roads with magnolia scented air. Spencer evokes affectionate reminisces of a past way of life. "Tiredness came with twilight," she remembers:

> 'Go take a bath before supper. Be sure and wash your feet.' The cook would have left dozens of biscuits in long pans ready for the oven, and there would be ham or a mountain of cold friend chicken, with potato salad, sliced tomatoes and cumbers, a wealth of peach preserves and blackberry jam, and tremendous appetites, much laughing and joking and good feelings, everybody cleaned up, the boys' hair slicked down with water. This was as good as it got (1996, 54).

Spencer's memories have more in common with country life as described by Garrison Keillor than with the America of that time described by Dreiser or Sinclair Lewis.

The two sides of her family, the Spencers and the McCains were of the genteel merchant class. "In my growing up time," Spencer writes (196, 8), "I thought of our two families, my mother's (the McCains) and my father's (the Spencers) as part of one, which was mine, and believed we were happy. I think that back then we mostly were." Her world is populated by loving kin. Grandfather Gan was (1996, 22) "the loving companion of days that would never be repeated." Uncle Sidney fixed "affectionate attentions" on his niece and was "ready to praise whatever good he could observe."

Even the racial system looks benign in retrospect. The South's code of apartheid was "an ugly system" she comments (1996, 32), "But in that childhood time of enchantment and love, it never seemed to be anything but part of the eternal. Might as well question why the live oaks were there, or the flowers in Aunt Ester's garden, or the stars in the sky." "As best I can recall" she writes about the relations of blacks to a beloved uncle, "they were exceptionally good-humored around him in a way that seemed to make their dependency a reassurance to them rather than a burden. I can't to this day believe I would not have noticed any deep-seated animosity." Later the Eden of childhood gives way to a more mature realization of what the polite south was really about, but the nostalgic images remain; "Enlightened as to its ills, as one would have to come to be, I could never deny that I loved it, or cease to look back on it with the greatest affection. I still claim joy as a good portion of its quality, and I love it still" (1996, 33).

As Coe notes, these reveries of a lost paradise are also realizations that modernity and progress have annihilated the pleasure and possibilities of the past. "This is more than nostalgia," he (1984, 64) writes, "it is nostalgia shot through with bitterness, resentment and disgust. Not merely – once upon a time – did the grass seem taller, the flowers and butterflies brighter, the birds noisier; it is a fact that there was once more grass and less concrete, that wildflowers and the butterflies had not yet been reduced to rarity by weedkillers and insecticides." In these memoirs, the outback is still pristine, major league baseball unsullied by free agency and corporate ownership, and the South beautiful and race relations harmonious. Basically, the message is the same in these memoirs. Something good that once existed has been destroyed.

What emerges from the memoirs considered here is the story of a child who is the incarnation of simplicity and innocence. They describe happy untroubled childhoods. They present a vision in which the child is the bearer of eternal verities. The child in paradise experiences a pure bliss that is not allowed to grown ups. The reason for this heightened sense of happiness is that the child has an undeveloped sense of time. These childhoods which never know the miseries described by McCourt and Karr et al. are privileged because they represent the hope of adults who see in the child the possibility for the fulfillment of their own dreams. That their youth will re-blossom in their old age.

Narratives of Childhood on Racial and Gender Borders

The new circumstances of childhoods lived in multicultural societies gives rise to a new type of childhood memoir. Aronowitz and Giroux (1991, 118-119) use the concept "border pedagogy," which sees cultural differences as enhancing public life and encouraging readers "to engage the multiple references that constitute different cultural codes, experiences, and languages including their own." There is a subgenre of memoir by biracial authors and gays about living on the borders of a race-obsessed and gender-obsessed society that allows readers to enter such a world of multiple references. A number of recent memoirs describe a childhood lived in a purgatory of sorts, a borderland—a social landscape in which children grow up on racial and gender borders, experiencing childhood in and between two social worlds. In these memoirs, identity is not established but in flux.

In *The Color of Water,* James McBride's moving narrative of his white mother's childhood as the daughter of a cruel itinerant Orthodox rabbi, and her efforts to put her dozen children through college, McBride recounts the multiple confusions of his own childhood with a white mother and twelve mixed race children in a black housing project surrounded by black people. Since conflict about racial identity was part of their lives "written into our very faces, hands and arms," McBride writes (1996, 94) "The question of race was like the power of the moon in my house. It's what made the river flow, the ocean swell, and the tide rise, but it was a silent power, intractable, indomitable, indisputable, and thus completely ignorable." But the question of race will not go away. "Is God black or white?," he asked his mother in frustration. In the answer (1996, 39) that gives the book its title, she said: "God's not black. He's not white…God is the color of water. Water doesn't have a color."

McBride's early childhood, in addition to containing all the ordinary joys and pangs and struggles of life in large family was touched by the confusions of living on the racial border—a black child with a white mother. At school, on the subway, at camp she was often "the only white face in a sea of black faces." His mother's whiteness often embarrassed and sometime alarmed him, for he perceived (1996, 5) her to be in "imminent danger from blacks and whites who disliked her for being a white person in a black world."

> I could see it in the faces of the white people who stared at me and Mommy and my siblings when we rode the subway, sometimes laughing at us, pointing, muttering things like, 'Look at her with those little niggers'…I remember two black women pointing at us, saying, "Look at that white bitch," and a white man screaming at Mommy somewhere in Manhattan, calling her a 'nigger lover' (1996, 23).

Such incidents confirmed his fears "that Mommy was always in danger." And there were other moments living on a racial border, living between two worlds: shopping with her black children and bargaining heatedly in Hasidic stores, his mother would suddenly shout in Yiddish, "I know what is happening here" when the merchants lapsed into Yiddish (1996, 66).

As a young adult McBride was torn between being a musician and a journalist, which he saw as a conflict between his blackness and his whiteness. That uncertainty set him tracing his Baptist minister father's heritage and learning about his mother's Jewish heritage. Although his mother is rejected by her Jewish family (they sit shiva for her) and she rejects them, she kept the Jewish passion for education and took advantage of the window of opportunity the education authorities granted to parents to have their children attend different school districts if they wanted. Consequently his mother "invariably chose predominantly Jewish public schools" (1996, 68). His experiences left him with a unique sensibility of life on a racial border. He describes himself living on a border, a black man with a Jewish soul:

> Now as a grown man, I feel privileged to have come from two worlds, My view of the world is not merely that of a black man but that of a black man with something of a Jewish soul. I don't consider myself Jewish, but when I look at Holocaust photographs of Jewish women whose children have been wrenched from them by Nazi soldiers, the women look like my mother and I think to myself, *There but for the grace of God goes my own mother—and by extension myself.* When I see two little Jewish old ladies giggling over coffee at a Manhattan diner, it makes me smile because I hear my own mother's laughter beneath theirs (79).

McBride explores his early confusion about race but never mentions feeling deprived or unhappy. He finds love and respect for both black and white worlds in his border experience.

In *Life on the Color Line* (1995) subtitled "the true story of a white boy who discovered he was black" Gregory Howard Williams tells his painful story of being brought up in Virginia believing that he was white and then moving to Indiana where he becomes "a colored boy." When his parent's marriage failed, Williams discovers that his father who had been passing for Italian was black. As the family split up, Gregory and his younger brother Mike return to Muncie, to live not with the white side of the family which lived in a sparkling new two story home they had visited previously, but with the black side of the family which had no indoor plumbing and used a slop jar on the porch.

William's literally lives on the border between the white and black world. "This is the projects" their father explained, "Colored families live on this side of Madison, and crackers on the other. Stay outta there. If the crackers learn you're colored, they'll beat the hell out of you. You gotta be careful here, too. Colored don't like half breeds either" (1995, 38). White relatives live only two miles away yet "not one of them had come for us" (1995, 51). Yet on the playground the black kids pick fights with him because he looks like a cracker. Williams is able explore issues of race and identity living on what he calls "the color line." The memoir balances the voice of the displaced boy with the calm voice of an adult which allows movement past the personal to the abstract. "Balancing on Muncie's racial tightrope," Williams (19995, 180) describes his experiences in school, sports, and dating. "Muncie would not permit me to date white girls," he notes, "and apparently couldn't tolerate seeing me with black girls either." (1995, 166) When he associates with white girl's coaches, counselors and teachers admonish him. When he is with black girls on the street and at school he is called a "nigger lover." Williams describes how, growing up as a mixed race child, he was often constrained by the "color line."

In the aptly titled *Black, White, and Jewish: the Autobiography of a Shifting Self* (2001), Rebecca Walker describes a childhood in a cultural trifecta. Walker examines the events and fragments of her childhood in the context of race and religion. The daughter of the novelist Alice Walker and the lawyer Mel Leventhal, Walker describes herself as a "Movement Child"—the offspring of a liberal white Jew who believed that equality and freedom could be achieved through law and an African American mother who believed that equality and freedom could be cultivated through the magic ability of words to redefine reality. Walker describes (2001, 12-13) her birth in Jackson Mississippi as: A mulatta baby swaddled and held in loving arms, two brown, two white, in the middle of the segregated South…That makes me the tragic mulatta caught between both worlds like the proverbial deer in the headlights." However, as she grew up, she notes, she never felt "contained," either by walls parents, or cultures. She lived in and moved back and forth between black, white, and Jewish communities.

After her parents divorced, she was raised by her parents in two-year shifts shuttling between coasts, her mother's San Francisco and her father's upper-middle class New York suburb. Ferrying between several worlds, she (2001, 117) grapples with where she fits in "Now as I move from place to place, from Jewish to black, from D.C. to San Francisco, from status quo middle class to radical artist bohemia, it is less like jumping from station to station on the radio dial and more like moving from planet to planet between universes that never overlap."

As an inquisitive child, a highly sensitive teen and a young woman, she is confronted with the color assumptions of friends, teachers and family. She describes how she is too white for blacks, and too black for whites. In elementary school, Bryan Katon tells her that he does not like black girls. She (2001, 93) takes ballet classes from a woman "who tells me I will never be a great ballerina because black women's bodies aren't suited for ballet." There have never been any famous black ballerinas. Visiting her mother's relatives in Atlanta an uncle (2001, 85) uses the word "cracker" "again and again to describe me or one of my mannerisms."

In junior high school, black girls threaten to beat her up for "acting like a white girl." In Larchmont, she attends a school where the black kids are "scruffy, unkempt and ashy, not mixing with "a sea of rich Jewish Kids." During the year she attended high school in Larchmont, not one black student says a word to her. At Fire Lake, a gauche Jewish camp where the campers obsessively listen to "Fiddler on the Roof," she is told she is too "intimidating." It doesn't occur to me," she notes, "that intimidating might be another word for black." (2001, 180) Later, after she is voted to be the captain of a singing programme by the girls, the counselors take away the honor because she is "too bossy, too tough." In high school, a boy friend criticizes her for being "too white."

Ultimately, Walker makes a choice between her shifting identities, choosing to "be on the right side of issues involving social justice." "In the twelfth grade," she (2001, 312) writes I decide to move Leventhal to the more obscure middle position in my name and add Walker to the end, privileging my blackness and downplaying what I think of as my whiteness." In *American Chica: Two Worlds, One Childhood*, (2002, 301), Marie Arana describes a childhood in which she is also shuttled between two deeply separate cultures for years. However, she comes to understand that she is a hybrid American—"a New World fusion, an American Chica." Arana focuses on the way culture not only divides and defines, but enriches.

Arana's memoir of growing up in Peru and America centers on her parents tumultuous marriage. She uses the metaphor of her parents' marriage to join North and South—chica and gringa. Her father, "a South American man," is an engineer. Her mother, "a North American woman," is a musician: "They were so different from each other, so obverse in every way." Yet their marriage survives 40 years, family difficulties, the politics of two continents and long separations. Their marriage overcomes bicultural tensions.

In her father's Peruvian family Arana was taught to be a proper lady, yet in her mother's family she learned to shoot a gun and break a horse. Her childhood is filled with the experience of living on cultural borders. In Peru, she learns about "Peruvian racism" when she is ostracized in a classroom for being too white: "I saw that Peru has its sediments too, and that its lines are drawn in color." (2001, 117) In the United States, she is seen as too black. When she visits her mother's family in Wyoming, an old man suggests that she and her brother are on the wrong side of town: "Suppose-ta be across those tracks over there on niggah side, ain'tcha now?" (2001, 192)

As a child, Arana is obsessed with the features of her physical composition. She contemplates the meaning of skin color in Peru and the United States. But after immigrating to the United States, she comes to understand, accept and appreciate that she is a hybrid. "I'm not any one thing," she (2001, 301) writes, "The reality is I am a mongrel. I live on bridges; I've earned my place on them, stand comfortably when I'm on one, content with betwixt and between." She counts both cultures as her own, and yet is caught between the two, celebrating being "a New World fusion. An American Chica."

Another type of border narrative involves gender. How do men whose erotic focus is other men shape the narrative of their childhood? How do women whose erotic interest is other women shape the narratives of their childhood?

In *Becoming A Man* (1992) Paul Monette describes the otherness of the conflicted life of a closeted gay childhood. Monette instructs (228) readers about his anguish as a gay boy who tried to be straight—to "pass," about "the process of 'de-selfing' my own world for the craziness that's turned my life into a minefield, this wanting to be somebody else instead of me." Monette confesses on the first page of his book that he grew up without a story of (gay) manhood that he could live by; "I was the only man I knew who had no story at all. I'd long since accepted the fact that nothing had ever happened to me and nothing ever would." Monette describes how he grew up in a "twilight world," a "hidden world," "turning "invisible," having to come "up with the right mask" (57) in order to be able to navigate through family and school. He describes hiding being gay in the role of the clown and the sophisticate. He also describes the safety zone of the courtier's role, "I came so close to being a eunuch escort full time".

Monette overtly uses literary language—images and analogies of being in the closet, of feeling oppression and suffocation, imagery of anguish about the conflict between private and the public self. Monette uses aggressive rhetoric to describe the closet. He describes how at nine and a half he had a physical relation with an male friend but is able to deny it's meaning; "That as long as I kept them apart, love would be sexless and sex loveless, endlessly repeating its cycle of self-denial and self-abuse. The process by which we become our own jailers, swallowing the key" (25). He lives a life of emotional solitude. Thus, by inexorable degrees does the love that dares not speak its name building walls instead, until a house is nothing but closets. This leads to his sexual arrested development; "that's where my sexuality stayed for the next twelve years, locked in the locker room of my brain." Emotional isolation, "consoling myself by means of connoisseurship for the bitter solitude of my life" (86).

In *Zami, A New Spelling of My Name* (1982) the poet Audre Lorde tells the story of an African-American lesbian life. Lorde says in the prologue to *Zami* that as a child she felt on the border between man and woman, that she had always wanted to be man and woman; "to incorporate the strongest and richest parts of my mother and father within/to share valleys and mountains upon my body the way the earth does in hills and peaks." In Greenwich Village she again stakes out a life on the border; "Downtown in the gay bars I was a closet student and an invisible black. Uptown at Hunter I was a closet dyke and general intruder."

Clearly, the sense of aloneness and separation felt by these authors is related to their search for individual identity. In these memoirs, the authors convey their consciousness of being alien, of being different, of being somehow wrong when they were children. Their narratives are self-examinations of growing up between two worlds, with attempts to retrace the steps that led from one world to another. Theirs is a search to explain the forging of an identity, for understanding of the present self in relation to the experience of having grown up betwixt and between and having crossed the borders of two social worlds.

Conclusion

The literary genre of the memoir has become a particularly robust trend in recent years. This new trend in confessional writing, the impetus to tell all has produced a virtual library of personal and sociological revelation. The memoir has opened up a new kind of narrative authority for the young, for ethnic and racial subcultures, for those of different sexual persuasions, and victims of abuse. In the closing decades of the twentieth century, there has been an outpouring of autobiographical writing by women and men focused on the urgent questions of identity and relationships.

In the closing decades of the twentieth century, there has been an outpouring of autobiographical writing by women and men focused on the urgent questions of identity and the significance and relevance of their childhoods. This chapter has attempted to examine some significant types of childhood that have been described in contemporary memoirs. If we look at this crop of memoirs as a group, some existential archetype attaches to each of them. The vision of childhood as a period of unmitigated suffering and abuse is most common. The depiction of the child as the victim of intrafamily conflicts and whose home life is transformed into a domestic hell by the cruelty of parents is a recurrent one. There are those memoirs that attempt to capture something of a paradise that has been lost, the once idyllic past where the child was happy and encapsulated in a protective cocoon, living in a loving and nurturing environment. The third existential archetype is of the child who does not fit in, a child without either disconnection or connection, but a search for connection. The narratives of biracial and gay childhoods describe a childhood between two worlds—white and black, Chica and American, gay and straight—where identity is not established, but in flux.

These childhood realms are resuscitated through memory. Constantly at work within the dynamics of these narratives depicting the state of childhood, there is a dialectical relationship between the present of adulthood and the past of childhood. The construction of these childhood worlds is not just an end in itself, but a pretext in service of a broader purpose. Those who recollect childhoods of misery use it as a framework for their own concerns with inadequate nurturing, the victimization of children and family breakup. Idyllic recreations may serve as an outlet for the nostalgia of the adult yearning after a long-lost paradise that may never have existed. Still another purpose that is served by the memoir is that of providing a convenient allegorical framework for the expression of certain political and philosophical viewpoints. The memoirs by biracial authors often use their childhood experience to make some statement on race and culture, as they see their lives testifying to the issue of race in America.

The story of childhood is one of the central themes in the current crop of memoirs. Among the many themes that writers have taken up in the recent memoir boom is the recollection of the experience of their childhoods. However, when memoirists speak of their childhoods, they do so through literary forms that seem to capture the universal archetypical forms of hell, heaven and a purgatory, a transitional stage of an ambiguous and conflicted social existence.

EPILOGUE

If the child was once ignored, on the margins of academic interests and kept on the fringe of social interaction, protected and out of sight in society, that has now changed. The significance of the child and childhood have become obvious in research on society and culture.

New and generative work has been and is being done by many scholars and researchers in history, social policy, psychology, and sociology. The child and childhood have become recognized as significant fields for analysis within professional organizations. A section on the "Sociology of Children" has been recognized by the American Sociological Association. A thematic group on the "Sociology of Childhood" has been recognized by the International Sociological Association.

The child and childhood have become salient political and social issues. Hillary Rodham Clinton wrote a best selling book, *It Takes a Village* which discusses the social importance of child and raising children. The theme of the 2000 Republican convention was "Leave No Child Behind." As noted, children have become increasingly assimilated into courtrooms. A concern for child-victims runs through recent American social reform. Both the Child Abuse Victims' Rights Act of 1986 and the Child Sexual Abuse and Pornography Act of 1986 became federal law. In New Jersey Megan's Law was passed in response to the tragic killing of Megan Kanka by a released sex offender. Megan's Law requires community notification that past sexual offenders are living in their midst. Legislation and policies to protect children from violence on television, pornography on the internet, and gun locks to prevent children from using guns are being considered.

The media highlights news that involves children. In addition to the stories discussed in Chapter Four, stories involving school shootings and bullying have been widely covered. Commercial films like "The Sixth Sense," "and Big Daddy," pair adult stars such as Adam Sandler and Bruce Willis with child actors in films in which there are adult child relationships. A number of recent films such as "Finding Neverland," "Little Miss sunshine," "The Martian Child," "About a Boy," and "Nim's Island" have featured story lines that have focused on the lives of children.

Currently a number of new issues involving the well being of children have come to the fore. As we have seen notions about what is "normal," and in a child's "best interest" have shifted over time, oftentimes in response to changes in production, consumerism, and human rights discourse. New issues and areas of research have recently been opened up in regard to the human rights of children. Since the essays that comprise Part I and Part II of this book were written, a number of scholars and authors concerned with the violation of the human rights of children have dealt with contemporary lost childhoods. Children have been separated out as a special case when dealing with economic, political, and social issues such as sexual exploitation and armed conflict in part by demonstrating the terrible impact of these phenomena on children, and by extension, older members of society as well. Advocates of child well being point to staggering statistics regarding the epidemic nature of human rights violations against children worldwide such as child labor, child prostitution, and child soldiery. Important recent research has focused on the lost childhoods of child laborers, child sex workers, and child soldiers. The following pages summarizes the extent of and the status of human rights violations against children

Child labor (Kenney, 2007) is the employment of children under an age determined by law or custom. The practice of child labor has come to be considered exploitative by many international organizations such as the United Nations and the International Labor Organization. The United Nations Convention on the Rights of the Child stipulates that:

> State parties recognize the right of the child to be protected from economic exploitation and from performing any work that is likely to be hazardous or to interfere with the child's education, or be harmful to the child's health or physical, mental, spiritual, moral or social development. (CRC, 1989)

In many countries (Kenney 2007, 3) constitutions and legislation prohibit work under specific ages, usually 16, and prohibit children working in hazardous or unhealthy work. However, a number of studies and reports find a chasm between the law and everyday practice.

The International Labor Organization (ILO) has estimated that 250 million children between the ages of five and fourteen work illegally in developing countries in industries as varied as agriculture, mining, ceramics, fireworks, deep-sea fishing, domestic services, and prostitution. At least 120 million children are working full time. According to the ILO sixty per cent of these are in Asia, thirty two percent are in Africa, and seven percent are in Latin America. Of the estimated 250 million children engaged in child labor around the world the vast majority---70 percent or some 170 million are working in agriculture. According to the ILO report on child labor, the number of children working in agriculture is nearly ten times that of children involved in factory work such as garment manufacturing, carpet weaving, and soccer ball stitching, activities which that have received attention. (Corsaro 2005)

In her study of child labor in Brazil Mary Lorena Kenny notes that in Brazil, over six million children between the ages of 5 and 9 are working in agriculture:

> About 60,000 children between the ages of 7-17 cut sugar cane in Pernambuco. They harvest coffee and bananas. They pick oranges in Sao Paulo for the multitude of juice we have. Employers like them because they are light and can climb trees without breaking branches. They pick cotton and sisal (jute) in Bahia for the rugs sold in places like Pottery Barn. (2007, 2)

In investigations in Egypt, Ecuador and India Human Rights Watch found that children working in agriculture were exploited on a daily basis. In Egypt Human Rights Watch examined the cotton industry where over one million children worked each year to manually remove pests from cotton plants. In Ecuador HRW found over 600,000 children working in banana fields and packing plants. In India they found over 15 million bonded children, most of them Dalits (untouchables) tending crops, herding cattle, and performing other tasks for their "masters."

Sex work is one of the most common forms of child labor. Child prostitution has come to forefront of global concerns, not only because of its recent growth, but also because of the growth of the international human rights movement. The ratification of the 1989 Convention on the rights of the Child has propelled child prostitution to the forefront of human rights attention. Child prostitution is found to effect millions of children and to be a gross violation of their rights and dignity, a practice that violates human rights standards not only of education and health, but also of the rights of children to be free from "exploitation" or "employment that may prove harmful to a child's moral development" (CRC, 1989).

Due to the clandestine nature of child prostitution and sex trafficking researchers must estimate and extrapolate the scale and the scope of the problem. Although attempts made to identify and study child prostitution around the world have many methodological problems, there is a consensus the number has been increasing. (Flowers, 1998; ECPAT, 2003; and Gathia, 1999). While some of the earliest research on child prostitution in developing countries began in the 1960's, the figures tracking a "rise" in child prostitution emerged in the early 1980's when NGO's began to invest energy and resources into fighting child prostitution. Arguably, the force of globalization has paradoxically helped to propel both the international success of the child's rights movement, and contributed to the rise in child prostitution.

In Southeast Asia alone, one study finds an estimated one million children are working as prostitutes (Gathia, 1999). Another study reports that there are a million child prostitutes in Thailand alone (Flowers, 1998). A recent study in the British medical journal The Lancet (2002) estimates that as many as two million children could be involved in child prostitution. Boys as well as girls are being prostituted, and according to the report, some of the children are as young as ten years old. They estimate the number of children exploited by prostitution is highest in India (400,000 to 575,000); Brazil is second (100,000 to 500,000); the United States is third (300,000); and in fourth place are Thailand and China (200,000) each.

Almost all the reports attribute the rise in the demand for child prostitutes to the increase in AIDS. The reason being that as the virus spreads around the world; people seek sexual partners who are unlikely to be infected. In the case of prostitution, children have become the targets of sexual exploitation because clients believe that rates of infection among children would likely be lower than those of adult prostitutes (Flowers, 1998). Females are also susceptible to the sex trade in that in traditional societies girls are often seen as less important than boys as potential contributors to the family. Females from remote areas, such as hill tribes in Thailand, or Nepal (for India), who come remote villages are viewed as unlikely to be HIV positive.

The title of the largest agency working to eradicate child prostitution, ÉCPAT— End Child Prostitution in Asian Tourism—insinuates that the source of the problem and the reason for its growth in Asia is tourism. A recent report from the ILO, "The Sex Sector: The Economic and Social Basis of Prostitution in Southeast Asia" found that in countries such as Thailand, Cambodia, and the Philippines, the "sex sector" accounts for anywhere between 2-14 percent of national income (qtd. in Klain, 1999, 37). Thus poverty provides a context in which children are highly vulnerable to exploitation. According to ECPAT, sex tourism is especially prevalent in Asia where in Cambodia one third of an estimated 800,000 prostitutes are children. Sex tourists travel to such countries to have sex with a child.

Although child sex tourism has existed for decades, the practice has exploded in recent years due to the rapid globalization of trade and the growth of the tourist industry. As countries once insulated now open their border to global markets, and as airfares become more affordable to travelers, sex offenders find new opportunities and easier means to travel abroad for underage sex. The rapid expansion of the internet has also fueled sex tourism by facilitating the distribution of child pornography and the advertising of sex tours.

The majority of sex tourists are adult males from more industrialized countries who travel to lesser developed countries where laws are non existent or not enforced, and sex is cheap and readily available. According to ECPAT Americans comprise 25% of sex tourists. Other major "source countries" include Japan and Australia.

Another form of child labor is children being used in armed conflict. Such children are denied a childhood and often subjected to horrific violence. A child soldier has been defined as a person under the age of 18 who directly or indirectly participates in an armed conflict as part of an armed force or group. While some children wield assault rifles, machetes, or rocket propelled grenades on the front lines others are used in "combat support" roles as messengers, spies, cooks, mine clearers, and some instances as sexual slaves. It is not uncommon, as recent testimony, such as Ishmael Beah contends, for them to participate in killing and raping.

The United Nations Convention on the Rights of the Child, Art 38, (1989) proclaimed: "State parties shall take all feasible measure to ensure that persons who have not attained the age of 15 years do not take a direct part in hostilities." According to Human Rights Watch children are direct participants in war in over twenty countries around the world. Human Rights Watch estimates that that around 300,000 children are serving as soldiers for rebel groups and government forces in armed conflict. These young combatants participate in all aspects of contemporary warfare. They wield AK-47's on the front lines and serve in a number of support roles such as lookouts and messengers.

As Ishmael Beah describes in his memoir, *A Long Way Gone: Memoirs of a Boy Soldier* (2007) children are uniquely vulnerable to military recruitment because of their emotional and physical immaturity. They are easily manipulated and can be channeled into violence that they are too young to resist or understand. Like Beah, many are abducted or recruited by force, and often compelled to follow orders under threat of death. Others join armed groups out of desperation. As society breaks down during conflict, children are separated from their homes. Beah describes his harrowing months fleeing the attack on his village by rebel soldiers in Sierra Leone. Many children see armed groups as their best chance of survival.

In his book *A Long Way Gone*, Ishmael Beah chronicles his life during the conflict in Sierra Leone. Thousand of children were recruited and used by all sides during Sierra Leones conflict from 1993-2002. As a young boy Beah gets swept away in Sierra Leone's civil war. Beah describes how he is transformed from a boy of twelve who is enthralled by American hip hop music and dance, and memorizes passages of Shakespeare into an internal refugee wandering from village to village after a rebel force destroyed his native village. After several months of flight he is forcibly recruited by the national army, and made into a soldier, learned to shoot an AK 47 and to hate and to kill the enemy. He is given drugs by the national army. "I smoked marijuana," he writes, "and snorted cocaine and *brown brown*." The result is that he and the other recruits are sleep deprived and easily manipulated. In the memoir Beah chronicles his life as a soldier. Unexpectedly running into another "armed group:"

We opened fire until the last living being in the outer group fell to the ground. We walked toward the dead bodies, giving each other high fives. The groups had also consisted of young boys like us, but we didn't care about them. We took their ammunition, sat on their bodies, and started eating the cooked food they had been carrying. All around us, fresh blood leaked from the bullet holes in their bodies. (2007, 19)

He describes how the army experience destroyed his innocence:

My squad was my family, my gun was my provider and protector, and my rule was to kill or be killed. The extent of my thoughts didn't go much beyond that. We had been fighting for over two years, and killing had become a daily activity. I felt no pity for anyone. My childhood had gone by without my knowing, and it seemed as if my heart had frozen. (2007, 126)

Beah's memoir provides a haunting picture of the life of a child soldier, and of how a gentle child can become a person capable of great brutalities.

At the beginning of the twenty first century the child has become established as a subject for research in many disciplines. As the previous chapters have noted the child has become a prominent subject for historians, social theorists, lawyers, the media, and students of popular culture. The once ignored child has become the obvious child. In addition to the child becoming the focus of societal and cultural attention, issues of child well being, retrieving the lost childhoods of child laborers, child sex workers, and child soldiers have become significant political issues in the world today.

Bibliography

Arana, Marie. *American Chica: Two Worlds, One Childhood*, New York: Random House, 2001.

Aries, Philippe. *Centuries of Childhood: A Social History*. New York: Random House, 1962.

Aronwitz, Stanley and Giroux, Henry, *Post Modern Education*. Minneapolis: University of Minnesota Press, 1991.

Atlas, James. "The Age of Memoir is Now," *The New York Times Magazine*, May 12, 1996.

Baxter, John. *Science Fiction in the Cinema*. New York: Paperback Library, 1970.

Beah, Ishmael. *A Long Way Gone*, New York: Farrar, Straus, and Giroux, 2007.

Bell, Daniel. *The Cultural Contradictions of Capitalism*. New York: Basic, 1976.

Bender, David & Leone, Bruno. *Child Abuse: Opposing Viewpoints*. San Diego: Greenhaven Press, Inc., 1994.

Benjamin, Walter. *Illuminations*. Edited by Hannah Arendt. New York: Schocken, 1973.

Bentovim, Arnon. *Child Sexual Abuse Within the Family*. London: Wright, 1988.

Berendzen, Richard. *Come Here*. New York: Villard, 1996.

Best, Joel. *Images of Issues* (ed) New York: Aldine de Gruyter, 1989.

Best, Joel. *Threatened Children: Rhetoric and concern About Child Victims*. Chicago: University of Chicago, 1990.

————----. *Troubling Children*. New York: Aldine de Gruyter, 1992.

Bettelheim, Bruno. *The Uses of Enchantment*. New York: Vintage, 1977.

Blais, Madeleine. "So You're Planning to Write Your Memoirs," *Nieman Reports*, Fall 1997.

Bolton, Ruthie. *Gal: A True Life*, New York: Hartcourt Brace and Company, 1994..

Boswell, John. *The Kindness of Strangers*. New York: Vintage, 1990.

Boulding, Kenneth. *The Meaning of the Twentieth Century*. New York: Harper and Row, 1964.

Brezezinski, Zbigniew. *Between Two Ages: America's Role in the Technocratic Era*. New York: Penguin, 1976.

Briskind, Peter. *Seeing is Believing: How Hollywood Taught Us to Stop Worrying and Love the Fifties*. New York: Pantheon, 1983.

Bronfenbrenner, Urie., Kessel, F., Kessen, W., and White, S. "Toward a Critical Social History of Developmental Psychology: A Propaedeutic Discussion," *American Psychologist*, 86: 1218–1230.

Brosnan, Joel. *Future Tense: The Cinema of Science Fiction*. New York: St. Martin's, 1978.

Brown, Norman. *Life Against Death*. Middletown: Wesleyan University Press, 1972.

Ceci, Stephen and Bruck Maggie. "Suggestibility of the Child Witness: A Historical Review and Synthesis." *Psychological Bulletin* (1993): 113:403–439.

Coe, Richard. *When The Grass Was Taller*. New Haven CT: Yale University Press. 1984.

Conway, Jill Kerr. *The Road From Coorain*, New York: Vintage. 1990.

Conway, Jill Kerr. *When Memory Speaks*, New York: Knopf. 1998.

Conrad, Peter and Schneider, J. *Deviance and Medicalization*. Philadelphia: Temple, 1992..

Cherlin, Andrew. *Public and Private Families 2nd edition*, New York: McGraw Hill, 1999.

Corsaro, William. *The Sociology of Childhood*. Thousand Oaks CA: Pine Forge, 1997.

Critser, Greg, *Fatland*, New York: Mariner Books, 2004

De Francis, Vincent *Protecting the Child Victime of Sex Crimes Committed by Adults*. Denver: American Humane Association, 1969.

de Mause, Lloyd. "The Evolution of Childhood." *The History of Childhood*. New York: Psychohistory Press (1974): 1–73.

Dent, Helen. "The effects of Age and Intelligence on Eyewitnessing Ability," in *Children as Witnesses*. Ed. By Helen Dent and Rona Flin. New York: John Wiley, 1992.

Dezwirek-Sas, Louise. "Empowering Child Witnesses for Sexual Abuse Prosecution," in *Children as Witnesses*, edited by Helen Dent and Rhona Flin. New York: John Wiley, 1992.

Dietz, W. and Gortmaker S., "Do We Fatten Our Children at the TV Set? Obesity and Television Viewing in Children and Adolescents," Pediatrics, 75 (1985): 807-812.

Dziech, Billie Wright and Schudson, Charles B. *On Trial: America's Courts and Their Treatment of Sexually Abused Children*. Boston: Beacon Press, 1989.

Eberele, Paul and Everle, Shirley. *The Abuse of Innocence: The McMartin Preschool Trial*. New York: Prometheus Books, 1993.

Elkind, David. *The Hurried Child*. Reading Mass: Addison-Wesley, 1981.

Erikson, Eric. *Childhood and Society*. New York: W. W. Norton, 1950.

Ferkiss, Victor. *Technological Man*. New York: New American Library, 1970.

Fiedler, Leslie. "Against the Cult of the Child." *Salinger*. ed. Henry A. Grunwald. New York: Harper, 1962. 218–45.

Finkelhor, David. "The 'Backlash' and the Future of Child Protection Advocacy: Insights from the Study of Social Issues," in *The Backlash: Child Protection Under Fire*, edited by John E. B. Myers. Thousand Oaks: Sage, 1994.

Finkelhor, David & Williams, Linda. *Nursery Crimes: Sexual Abuse in Day Care*. Newbury Park: Sage, 1988.

Flin, Rhona; Bull, Ray; Boon, Julian; and Knox, Anne. "Children in the Witness-Box," in *Children as Witnesses*. edited by Helen Dent and Rhona Flin. New York: Wiley, 1992.

Freud, Sigmund. "The contributions to the theory of sex," in A. A. Brill (ed.) *The Basic Writings of Sigmund Freud*, Book III. New York: Modern Library, 1938.

———. *The Interpretation of Dreams*, trans. A. H. Brill, London: George Allen and Co., 1913.

———. *Leonardo da Vinci and a Memory of His Childhood*. New York: W. W. Norton, 1964a.

————. *The Future of Illusion*, trans. W. D. Robson Scott. New York: Anchor, 1964b.

Frith, Simon. *Sound Effects*. New York: Pantheon, 1981.

Fromm, Erich. *The Revolution of Hope*. New York: Harper and Row, 1974.

Gasset, Ortega. Y. *Toward a Philosophy of History*. New York: W. W. Norton, 1941.

Gilbert, Dennis. *The American Class Structure 5ᵗʰ edition*. New York: Wadsworth Publishing Co. 1998.

Goodman, G. "The Child Witness: An Introduction." *Journal of Social Issues* (1984): 40(2), 1–7.

Goodman, Paul. *Growing Up Absurd*. New York: Vintage, 1960.

————. "Reflections on Children's Rights," in *The Children's Rights Movement*, edited by B. Gross and R. Gross. New York: Doubleday, 1977.

Goodwin, Doris Kearns. *Wait Till Next Year*. New York: Simon and Schuster, 1997.

Gordon, Mary. *The Shadow Man*. New York: Random House. 1996.

Gornick, Vivian. "The Memoir Boom" *The Women's Review of Books*. 13, 5.

Gortmaker, S., Must,A., Sobel, A., Peterson, K., Colditz, S and Dietz, W., "Television Viewing as a Cause of Increasing Obesity among Children in the United states, 1986-1990," *Archives of Pediatrics & Adolescent Medicine* 150 (April 19960): 356-362.

Gornick, Vivian. "The Memoir Boom," *The Women's Review of Books*, July 1996.

Grass, Gunter. *The Tin Drum*. Trans. Ralph Manheim. New York: Pantheon, 1959.

Green, Germaine. *Sex and Destiny*. New York: Harper and Row, 1982.

Grubb, Norton, and Lazerson Marvin. *Broken Promises*. New York: Basic, 1982.

Hampl, Patricia. *I Could Tell You Stories: Sojourns in the Land of Memory*, New York: W.W. Norton, 1999.

Handle, Gerald, et.al., *Children and Society*, Los Angeles: Roxbury Publishing, 2007.

Hechler, David. *Lawyers for Children: No Experience Necessary*. Washington D. C. Justice for Children, 1985.

————. *The Battle and the Backlash: The Child Sexual Abuse War.*
    Massachusetts: Lexington Books, 1988.
Holstein, Joel.A. and Miller Gale. (eds) *Reconsidering Social
    Constructionism,* New York: Aldine de Gruyter, 1993.
Horkheimer, Max. *Eclipse of Reason,* New York: Seabury, 1977.
————. "The End of Reason," *Studies in Philosophy and Social Science,
    #9.* 1941.
Karr, Mary. *The Liar's Club: A Memoir.* New York: Penguin. 1995.
Kirsh, Steven J. *Children, Adolescents, and Media Violence,* Thousand
    Oaks: Sage Publications, 2006.
Kohlberg, Lawrence. *Collected Papers on Moral Development and Moral
    Education.* Cambridge Mass: Center for Moral Education, 1973.
Kozol, Jonathan. *Savage Inequalities,* New York: Harper Perennial, 1991.
Kroll, Jack. "Close encounters of the third kind: The UFO's are coming."
    Newsweek (November 21): 82.
Kuhn, Reinhold. *Corruption in Paradise: The Child in Western
    Literature.* Hanover N.H.: University Press of New England, 1982.
Lears, Jackson. *No Place of Grace: Antimodernism and the
    Transformation of American Culture 1800–1920.* New York:
    Pantheon, 1981.
Linn, Susan. *Consuming Kids,* New York: Anchor Books, 2004.
Locke, John. *The Educational Writings of John Locke.* Edited by J.
    Adamson. London: Cambridge University Press, 1922.
Loftus, Elizabeth. "Leading Questions and the Eyewitness Report," in
    Cognitive Psychology (1975): 7, 560–572.
Lorde, Audre. *Zami: A New Spelling of My Name.* Freedom, CA:The
    Crossing Press. 1982.
Lurie, Alison. *Don't Tell the Grown-Ups.* New York: Avon, 1990.
Mailer, Norman. *Advertisements for Myself.* New York: Berkley, 1959.
Marcus, Greil. *Mystery Train: Images of America in Rock'n Roll Music.*
    New York: Dutton, 1975.
Marcuse, Herbert. *Eros and Civilization.* New York: Vintage, 1962.
"Michael's World." *Newsweek* 6 Sept. 1993: 34–38.
McBride, James. *The Color of Water.* New York: Riverhead Books, 1996..
McCourt, Frank, *Angela's Ashes,* New York: Scribner, 1996.
Monette,Paul. *Becoming a Man.* San Franciso: Harper Collins, 1992.

Mungo, Raymond. *Total Loss Farm*. New York: Dutton, 1970.

Myers, John E. B. *Child Witness: Law and Practice*. New York: John Wiley & Sons, 1987.

———. "Definition and Origins of the Backlash Against Child Protection," *The Backlash: Child Protection Under Fire*, edited by John E. B. Myers. Thousand Oaks: Sage, 1994.

———. *Legal Issues in Child Abuse and Neglect*, Newbury Park: Sage Publications.

———. "The Sexual Abuse Literature: A Call for Greater Objectivity," *The Michigan Law Review (1990)*. Vol. 88. 1709–1733.

Nelson, B. J. *Making an Issue of Child Abuse: Political Agenda Setting for Social Problems*. Chicago: University of Chicago Press, 1984.

Neustadter, Roger. "'Killing Babies:' The Use of Image and Metaphor in the Right-to-Life Movement," *Michigan Sociological Review*, No. 4, Fall, 1990.

———. "Fetal Attraction: Legal, Ethical, and Sociological Considerations in the Criminalization of Pregnancy," Journal of Crime and Justice, Vol. XVII, No. 2, 1994.

———. "The Emergence of Recovered Memory as a Social Problem," in *Counseling and the Therapeutic State*, ed. James Chriss, New York: Aldine de Gruyter, 1999.

Newsweek, March 21, 1994.

Newsweek, December 1, 1997.

Newsweek, April 10, 2000.

Nicholson, Gordon, Murray Kathleen. *Children as Witnesses*, edited by Helen Dent and Rhona Flin. New York: John Wiley, 1992.

O'Connor, Flannery. *Mystery and Manners*. New York: Noonday Press. 1969.

Packard, Vance. *Our Endangered Children*. Boston: Little and Brown, 1983.

Parsons, Talcott. *Social Structure and Personality*. New York: Free Press, 1965.

———. "The Social Structure of the Family," in *The Family, Its Functions and Destiny*, edited by R. N. Anshen. New York: Harper, 1959.

———. *The Social System*. New York: Free Press, 1964.

Pfhol, Stephen. "The Discovery of Child Abuse," *Social Problems* (1977). V. 24, 310–321.

Piaget, Jean. *Genetic Epistemology*. New York: W. W. Norton, 1970.

———. *Psychology and Epistemology*. New York: Viking Press, 1975.

———. *The Child's Conception of Time*. New York: Ballantine Books, 1971.

Platt, Anthony. *The Child Savers*. Chicago: University of Chicago Press, 1969.

Pleck, Elizabeth. *Domestic Tyranny*. New York: Oxford University Press, 1987.

Pollitt, Katherine. "Tyranny of the Fetus," *New Statesman and Society*, March 1990.

Pogrebin, Letty Cottin. "Do Americans Hate Children?" *Ms.* Nov. 1983: 47–50.

Postman, Neil. *The Disappearance of Childhood*. New York: Dell, 1982.

Rawson, Beryl. "Children in the Roman Familia." *The Family in Ancient Rome: New Perspectives*. Ithaca: Cornell University Press (1986): 170–200.

Redfield, Robert. *The Primitive World and Its Transformation*. Ithaca: Cornell, 1953.

Rhoades, Richard. *A Hole in the World: An American Boyhood*. New York: Touchstonre, 1990.

Roth, Henry. *Call It Sleep*. New York: Avon, 1965.

Rostow, Walt. W. *The Stages of Economic Growth*. London: Cambridge University Press, 1960.

Rousseau, Jean. Jacques. *Emile, Julie and Other Writings*. New York: Barrons Educational Series, 1964.

Roszak, Theodore. *Unfinished Animal*. New York: Harper Colophon, 1975.

Schachtel, Ernst. G. *Metamorphosis*. New York: Basic Books, 1959.

Schlesinger, Arthur. *The Vital Center*. Boston: Houghton Mifflin Co., 1962.

Schroyer, Trent. *The Critique of Dominations*. Boston: Beacon Press, 1973.

Shorter, Edward. *The Making of the Modern Family*. New York: Basic Books, 1977.

Singal, D. J. "Towards a Definition of American Modernism," *American Quarterly* (1987) 87:7–26.

Sommerville, C. John. *The Rise and Fall of Childhood*. New York: Vintage, 1990.

Spector, Malcolm. and Kituse, John. *Constructing Social Problems*, Menlo Park, CA: Benjamin Cummings, 1977.

Spencer, Elizabeth. *Landscapes of the Heart*, New York: Random House. 1996.

Spencer, John. R. "Reforming the Law on Children's Evidence in England: The Pigo Committee and After," in *Children as Witnesses*, edited by Helen Dent and Rhona Flin. New York: John Wiley, 1992.

Stein, Gertrude. *Everybody's Autobiography*, New York: Vintage. 1996.

Stone, Lawrence. *The Massacre of Innocent*. New York Review of Books: November 14 (1974): 25–31.

Stone, Lawrence. *The Family, Sex, and Marriage In England 1500–1800*. New York: Harper Colophon Books, 1979.

Sutton-Smith, B. "Piaget on Play: A Critique," in *Child's Play*, edited by B. Sutton-Smith. New York: John Wiley and Sons, 1971.

Suransky, Valerie. *The Erosion of Childhood*. Chicago: University of Chicago Press, 1985.

Tawney, R. H. *Religion and the Rise of Capitalism*. New York: Harcourt Brace and Co., 1926.

Vonnegut, Kurt. *Slaughter House Five*. New York: Dell, 1969.

Wager, Warren. *Good Tidings*. Bloomington: Indiana University Press, 1972.

Wakefield, Hollida and Underwager, Ralph. *Accusations of Sexual Abuse*. Illinois: Charles C. Thomas, 1988.

Walker, Rebecca. *Black, White, and Jewish: Autobiography of a Shifting Self.* New York: Vintage. 2001

Wattenberg, Ben. *The Birth Dearth*. New York: Pharos, 1987.

Wexler, Richard. *Wounded Innocents: The Real Victims of the War Against Child Abuse*. New York: Prometheus Books, 1990.

Whitcomb, Debra. "Legal Reforms on Behalf of Child Witnesses: Recent Developments in the American Courts," in *Children as Witnesses*, edited by Helen Dent and Rhona Flin. New York: John Wiley, 1992.

Williams, Gregory Howard. *Life on the Color Line*. New York: Plume, 1995.

Wimberly, Lesley. "The Perspective From Victims of Child Abuse Laws (VOCAL)," in *The Backlash: Child Protection Under Fire*, edited by John E. B. Myers. Thousand Oaks: Sage, 1994.

Winn, Marie. *Children Without Childhood*. New York: Penguin, 1983.

Wright, Lawrence. *Remembering Satan*. New York: Knopt, 1994.

Yapko, Michael. *Suggestions of Abuse*. New York: Simon and Schuster, 1994.

Zelizer, Viviana A. *Pricing the Priceless Child: The Changing Social Value of Children*. New York: Basic Books, 1985.